Presented to

From

Date

A Mustard Seed

FAITH

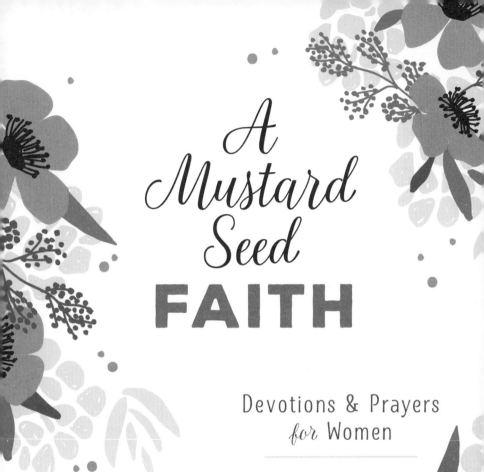

A Mustard Seed FAITH

Devotions & Prayers for Women

CAREY SCOTT

BARBOUR
PUBLISHING

ISBN 978-1-64352-962-2

Published by Barbour Publishing, Inc., 1810 Barbour Drive, Uhrichsville, Ohio 44683, www.barbourbooks.com

Our mission is to inspire the world with the life-changing message of the Bible.

ecpa Member of the
Evangelical Christian
Publishers Association

Printed in China.

TINY FAITH CAN MOVE MOUNTAINS!

*"Truly I tell you, if you have
faith as small as a mustard seed,
you can say to this mountain,
'Move from here to there,' and it will move.
Nothing will be impossible for you."*
MATTHEW 17:20 NIV

Faith empowers our relationship with God, yet we often think what little we have isn't enough to matter. We compare ourselves to others and are left feeling like our tiny faith is worthless. But God knew we'd need encouragement to believe the size of our faith is enough. And He promises that time spent with Him will grow it even more, deepening its roots in our heart.

In the pages of this book, women of all ages will find much-needed encouragement to be faith-filled lovers of Jesus. This beautiful devotional offers the inspiration and biblical truth they need to deepen their trust in Him. Through the journey of 180 full-length devotional readings, women will find topics important to their heart, including God's faithfulness, God's love, fear, insecurity, uncertainty, worthlessness, anxiety, doubt, trust, wisdom, prayer, and more. By the end, the reader will have a greater appreciation of the power and potential of faith in her life.

THE POWER OF IF

Jesus replied, "Listen to the truth. If you have no doubt of God's power and speak out of faith's fullness, you can be the ones who speak to a tree and it will wither away. Even more than that, you could say to this mountain, 'Be lifted up and be thrown into the sea' and it will be done. Everything you pray for with the fullness of faith you will receive!"

MATTHEW 21:21–22 TPT

This is a powerful concept. Don't miss the "if" opportunity in Jesus' words. He is encouraging you to pray with the fullness of faith and emboldening you to cast aside doubt. And the Lord is empowering you to tap into God's abilities to give you what you need in the moment. *If* you choose to believe in the Lord's promise and embrace His authority in your situation, and *if* you command in His name, your faith has the capacity to shift things.

Pray with fervor when you need God's help, and then decide to believe God hears you and will show up. Why? Because your faith matters to the Father, and He will bless you for it.

Father, I know I have a choice to activate my faith in You or not. I know that I can try to fix things on my own or trust in You. Please increase my faith in the power of "if," believing that it allows me to tap into Your strength and power. In Jesus' name I pray, amen.

ARE YOU LISTENING?

The point is: Before you trust, you have to listen. But unless Christ's Word is preached, there's nothing to listen to.

ROMANS 10:17 MSG

Sometimes it feels like we are too busy to stop and listen for God's voice. We look at our endless to-do list, put our nose to the grindstone, and power through it. We get distracted by the fight we had with our husband this morning, the whining kids in the backseat, or the boss who thinks we are superwoman and piles the work on. We ruminate over the offending words, get stuck replaying the injustice, or strategize our revenge instead of asking the Lord to speak in our situation.

For you to trust that God will intervene, you have to hear His promises. You have to listen to reminders that He loves you and is always for you. You must recite the verses He has laid on your heart. Friend, you need a booster shot of His faithfulness before you will feel comfortable prying your hands off the wheel so He can slide into the driver's seat. In the middle of your mess, are you listening for God?

Father, I confess that I get too busy sometimes to include You in my everyday struggles. Forgive me for trying to do life alone. From today on, I promise to be intentional to listen for Your voice and remember Your Word as faith-building opportunities. In Jesus' name I pray, amen.

GET OFF THE FENCE

But without faith it is impossible to [walk with God and] please Him,
for whoever comes [near] to God must [necessarily] believe that God exists
and that He rewards those who [earnestly and diligently] seek Him.
HEBREWS 11:6 AMP

When you're in a relationship with someone, you want to make them happy. You want to learn about them—their cares, concerns, and celebrations—so you can better understand them. It's important to spend time with them to grow closer. You start trusting them, and they you. These steps are vital in establishing a healthy connection to someone you care about, right?

Remember investing your time and trust in the Lord is also indispensable. That relationship is what empowers you to live a faith-filled life. And without a strong faith in God, it's impossible to please Him. When you're on the fence about the Lord, it keeps you from digging deeper with Him. But when you embrace your faith and trust in God—seeking Him every day—you will be blessed in countless ways beyond imagination.

Father, I just want You to know that I am all in. I am off the fence once and for all! And I am going to richly invest in our relationship because I want to make You happy. I want to know You better. Because I know that when I focus on growing with You, life will be full of beautiful things. In Jesus' name I pray, amen.

YOUR HANDLE

The fundamental fact of existence is that this trust in God, this faith,
is the firm foundation under everything that makes life worth living.
It's our handle on what we can't see. The act of faith is what
distinguished our ancestors, set them above the crowd.
HEBREWS 11:1–2 MSG

Let your faith be the firm foundation for your life. Let it be what sustains you when you're weary. Let it be what you hold on to when life becomes tornadic. Let faith be the reason for the peace you feel in the midst of chaos. Let it be why you don't give up or give in when everything seems to be falling apart. Allow faith to be what drives you to get back up and try again. And let it be the handle you cling to when you're desperate for hope and help.

Faith is hard to walk out sometimes. It requires grit to choose it over fear. And the world encourages you to rely on yourself or others instead of the Lord. But friend, it's trusting in God that makes life worth living because you come alive as you draw close to your Creator. Faith is your handle. Grab onto it!

Father, I know being full of faith is hard at times. Too often I think I can
figure it all out. But I want You to be my firm foundation and the handle
I choose to cling to every day. In Jesus' name I pray, amen.

IT'S YOUR MUSTARD SEED FAITH

For it's by God's grace that you have been saved. You receive it through faith. It was not our plan or our effort. It is God's gift, pure and simple. You didn't earn it, not one of us did, so don't go around bragging that you must have done something amazing.

Ephesians 2:8–9 voice

What a wonderful reminder that it's your faith—your belief in the Lord—that secures you a place in heaven. Honestly, it should be a big sigh of relief to know you don't have to live up to certain standards or complete a checklist of accomplishments. You're not required to act a certain way, recite magical words, or perform sacred rituals as an entrance fee. Your eternity wasn't guaranteed because of anything you did to earn it. Instead, revel in the sweet truth that it's because of God's grace you've been saved. It's your mustard seed faith in action that makes an eternal life with God possible.

Be careful you don't brag about your works, telling others you earned your spot with the Almighty. Instead, humbly thank Him for loving you enough to make eternity a reward for simply believing.

Father, I am so glad You don't expect my actions to secure heaven for myself. I'd be in a world of hurt. While I know my eternity is settled, help me live a life worthy of You. Give me courage to be bold in my faith. In Jesus' name I pray, amen.

MUSTER UP A LITTLE FAITH

"Not one promise from God is empty of power,
for nothing is impossible with God!"
LUKE 1:37 TPT

It takes a strong resolve to believe today's verse. We have to cling to this truth when our marriage is falling apart, and we don't see the path to reconciliation. We have to hold it tight when our kids are making choices that don't line up with who we know them to be. We must white knuckle it when the diagnosis looks bleak, the finances are overwhelming, and our best friend betrays our trust. It's vital we remember that situations that look hopeless in the natural are never hopeless in the spiritual.

The truth is that you were never meant to figure everything out on your own. You don't have to navigate this life alone. We need God's help to walk out this life well. And we don't have to be pillars in the faith to get His help. Friend, even if you can muster up a little faith, take it to the Lord and ask for help. It will always come.

Father, what a blessing that I am not required to fix everything myself. What a relief that I don't have to live in a hopeless state. And what an awesome promise that when I reach the end of me, You are there. Thank You for being the God of possible. I can't imagine living without You. In Jesus' name I pray, amen.

YOU'RE INVITED

Now on the final and most important day of the Feast, Jesus stood, and He cried in a loud voice, If any man is thirsty, let him come to Me and drink! He who believes in Me [who cleaves to and trusts in and relies on Me] as the Scripture has said, From his innermost being shall flow [continuously] springs and rivers of living water.
JOHN 7:37–38 AMPC

Did you know that you've been invited into a relationship with the Lord? Just like Jesus did at the Feast, He calls out to you, offering to meet every need you have in life. He wants to be the One who sustains, heals, and rescues you. The Lord wants to be the One who encourages and guides you. Have you heard Him? Even more, have you answered?

In this crazy world, how wonderful to know we have a God who sees us right where we are. How amazing to commune with a God who offers to quench a thirst that only He can satisfy. When you choose to cling to God, trust His will and ways and rely on Him for the outcome. You will find peace, strength, and wisdom.

Father, what a privilege to be called into a relationship with You! Thank You for inviting me into community. I energetically say yes, and I ask that You help me believe in Your promises and trust in them. In Jesus' name I pray, amen.

ASK GOD FOR
WHAT YOU NEED

*This is My command: be strong and courageous. Never be afraid
or discouraged because I am your God, the Eternal One,
and I will remain with you wherever you go.*

JOSHUA 1:9 VOICE

Sometimes we need an extra measure of bravery to make it through. Life has a crazy way of throwing curve balls when we least expect it, doesn't it? And they can leave us scared because we were knocked off balance and everything feels out of control. At the end of the day, it really does matter knowing we're not standing alone. It helps knowing we have a God who will meet us in our fear.

It's in these moments God's presence means so much. He's the One we ask for what we need to navigate the choppy waters ahead. When a hard conversation with someone we love is on the horizon, ask for the courage to be honest. When you're facing change, ask for fearless faith as you trust Him. When you're hurting and want to quit, ask God for the confidence to continue.

*Father, sometimes it's hard to admit I need Your help because I feel equipped
in my own strength. I feel like You made me able to handle anything that comes
my way. But I'm learning how much I need Your help, especially in those times
where I feel overwhelmed and afraid. What a relief to know I don't have
to have all the answers. Thank You. In Jesus' name I pray, amen.*

COMPLETELY RELY

Place your trust in the Eternal; rely on Him completely; never depend upon your own ideas and inventions. Give Him the credit for everything you accomplish, and He will smooth out and straighten the road that lies ahead.

Proverbs 3:5–6 voice

Let's be honest. It's a tall order to *completely* rely on the Lord. It's not that He's unable to do what needs to be done, but it's our inability to give up control that makes this so hard to do. We may know God always wants the best for us, but we worry His best and our desire may not be the same. We may believe He is capable, but what if His timing doesn't line up with ours? And even more, we may have a track record of good choices and solid decisions, so suggesting we cannot depend on ourselves feels crazy.

This is a radical step of faith, but you can trust an unknown future to a known God. When you walk this out, you're choosing to surrender. You are telling the Lord you trust His ways over yours. And with each step forward, it keeps you open to letting God course correct if needed.

●

Father, I confess there are times I struggle to completely rely on You. Sometimes I have a crisis of faith and get impatient. I hold on to my plans tighter than I should. Help me build up my confidence in You. In Jesus' name I pray, amen.

PRAYING WITH GREAT FAITH

*I pray with great faith for you, because I'm fully convinced that
the One who began this glorious work in you will faithfully
continue the process of maturing you and will put his finishing
touches to it until the unveiling of our Lord Jesus Christ!*

PHILIPPIANS 1:6 TPT

In today's verse, Paul shares that he was able to pray with *great faith* because he was completely convinced that God would keep His promises without fail. He decided to believe the Lord could and would. And Paul chose to trust that He wouldn't give up and walk away from the perfecting work He was doing. So instead of giving in to doubt, Paul kept his eyes on God.

How would your situation change if you had the same response? What if the words you spoke about the difficult circumstance revealed no reservation, and instead pointed to the unwavering trust you had in God? What if you shut down any skeptical or worrisome thoughts by opening the Bible to belief-building scriptures? You know, even a small step in the direction of faith yields big results in God's economy. And every time you say yes and believe, the Lord will honor it.

•

*Father, help me be the kind of woman who prays with great faith.
Give me the courage to trust in You when something seems impossible.
I know the Word says You always keep Your promises, but sometimes
doubt creeps in. Help my unbelief. In Jesus' name I pray, amen.*

NOT BY SIGHT

*For we walk by faith, not by sight [living our lives in a
manner consistent with our confident belief in God's promises].*
2 Corinthians 5:7 amp

Think about how painful it is to sit and ruminate over a heartbreaking situation. When we obsess over the scary circumstances we're facing, it overwhelms us with a sense of dread. When someone we love deploys, we feel helpless. When our finances crater, we feel defenseless. When our health falters, we feel hopeless. And if we spend our time looking at these kinds of things, they will eventually take us out.

Instead, God invites you to keep your eyes on Him and bring your anxious heart to Him in prayer when fear creeps in, rather than spiraling into depression. It means opening your Bible to find peace rather than trying to numb yourself with food or shopping. It means speaking out *I trust You* when the tornados of life start swirling around, and you can't make sense of it all. It means you choose to believe that God is good, that He loves you, and that He will fulfill every promise He made. Faith is a choice—it's always a choice. Choose wisely.

*Father, sometimes I choose to manage my life rather than trust You.
Help me walk in the unwavering belief that I can be confident in
Your love and goodness for all things. In Jesus' name I pray, amen.*

YOUR RESPONSE
IS FAITH

"This is how much God loved the world: He gave his Son, his one and only Son. And this is why: so that no one need be destroyed; by believing in him, anyone can have a whole and lasting life."

JOHN 3:16 MSG

Because the Lord loves us too much to fathom, He took radical action to set things right. The moment Adam and Eve disobeyed, sin entered the world. And because God is holy, it separated us from Him. To the Lord, this was unacceptable, so He set into motion drastic measures to ensure there would be no barriers between us. He devised a beautiful plan of salvation accessible to anyone who chooses it. That includes you.

Friend, faith is your response to God's selfless gift of His Son. You don't need a boatload of belief to walk this out. You don't have to be a pillar of faith or have your life cleaned up. There's nothing you can do to make yourself sinless. It's not up to you to earn your way into heaven. What is required of you is enough faith to believe Jesus gave His life at the Father's request to erase your sin. That small *yes* is a seed of faith He will grow daily.

Father, thank You for Jesus. I'm so grateful I don't have to find a way to earn an eternity with You. Help my faith continue to grow in You! In Jesus' name I pray, amen.

FAITH IN ACTION

My brothers and sisters, what good is it if people say they have faith but do nothing to show it? Claiming to have faith can't save anyone, can it? Imagine a brother or sister who is naked and never has enough food to eat. What if one of you said, "Go in peace! Stay warm! Have a nice meal!"? What good is it if you don't actually give them what their body needs? In the same way, faith is dead when it doesn't result in faithful activity.

James 2:14–17 CEB

We are compelled, even if our faith is small, to let it show. It's not because we want to be prideful, boasting that we are better. It's not that we believe we work our way to heaven. But instead, it's out of the overflow of joy and gratitude that we want to bless others. It could be as small as offering to help someone move to generously donating to a cause close to our heart. It may be volunteering our time or sharing the Gospel in a third world country. The truth is that there's no way you can have faith in God and not want to act out of it.

●

Father, open my heart to live with generosity and kindness toward those around me. Let me make a difference for Your kingdom. Fill me with confidence to walk out my faith every day. In Jesus' name I pray, amen.

BOLD PRAYERS

*Just make sure you ask empowered by confident faith without
doubting that you will receive. For the ambivalent person believes
one minute and doubts the next. Being undecided makes you
become like the rough seas driven and tossed by the wind.
You're up one minute and tossed down the next.*

JAMES 1:6 TPT

When you take a request to the Lord, be bold. Audaciously ask Him for what you need. You don't have to plead or beg. You don't have to have the right words or be sinless. You don't need to crawl in shame and ask for His help. But you do have to ask in faith, choosing to believe that God can do whatever you need.

Here's where we get messed up. When He doesn't answer us in our time frame or in the way we want Him to respond, we assume He can't. We assume He won't. And so, we stop asking and handle things on our own. Part of having faith means trusting that God's will and timing are perfect, and that while He hears our prayers, He loves us enough to answer according to His plan for our life. Let's decide to courageously ask and then accept how and when He answers. That's faith.

●

*Father, give me bold faith to ask for what I need and surrendering faith
to accept Your answer. Help me believe that You're always on my side,
cheering me on every day. In Jesus' name I pray, amen.*

SEASONS

I know what it means to lack, and I know what it means to experience
overwhelming abundance. For I'm trained in the secret of overcoming
all things, whether in fullness or in hunger. And I find that the strength
of Christ's explosive power infuses me to conquer every difficulty.
PHILIPPIANS 4:12–13 TPT

The truth is that life is full of seasons, amen? Some are so epic. Everything seems to be going your way. Your relationships are strong, your finances are secure, your health is shipshape, and all feels right in the world. You wake every day with a smile and jump from bed ready for more awesomeness. But then comes the next season where you want to hide in bed with a pint of your favorite ice cream.

In this season nothing comes together, and you're trying to keep broken plates spinning. It feels like everything that could go wrong. . . does. Life is full of chaos and frustration, and you're waving the white flag of surrender. You want off the ride.

Either way, let your faith remain the same. It's easy to cling to God when the hard times hit but then shove Him aside when things are drama-free. Choose to be the kind of woman who recognizes the need for God regardless of the season.

Father, I want You in my life when it's hard and easy. I want to
grow in our relationship through the thick and thin. Let my
faith be solid through it all. In Jesus' name I pray, amen.

ASK FOR AN INCREASE

"No matter how many times in one day your brother sins against you and says, 'I'm sorry; I am changing; forgive me,' you need to forgive him each and every time." Upon hearing this, the apostles said to Jesus, "Lord, you must increase our measure of faith!"

LUKE 17:4–5 TPT

To some, this verse offers a little levity because it shows how very human the apostles were. Can you hear the desperation in their response? Jesus' suggestion was a weighty one, and maybe they felt it was almost impossible to walk out. But rather than shaking their heads and walking away, they knew their only hope of obeying was asking Him to increase their level of faith.

You can do the same thing. When you need strength for the hard conversation. . .when you need wisdom to know the next step. . .when you need grace to let the offense go. . .when you need courage to stand up for truth. . .ask the Lord to increase your faith. When you're struggling to trust that God will show up, ask for an increase. When it seems things will never change, ask for an increase. The gift of more is always available—just ask.

Father, I can think of so many places in my life I need more faith. There are hard situations that are too big for my human condition. And I am asking that You would give me the ability to believe You will intervene. In Jesus' name I pray, amen.

HELP MY LITTLE FAITH

*Jesus said to him, "What do you mean 'if'? If you are able to believe,
all things are possible to the believer." When he heard this, the boy's
father cried out with tears, saying, "I do believe, Lord; help my little faith!"*

MARK 9:23-24 TPT

Have you ever felt like your faith wasn't good enough? Maybe you've looked at others who have been through so much and their faith remained intact. Maybe it even grew stronger through the battle. You watched as they walked through some of the hardest times with confidence that God would be big in their circumstances. And maybe it made you wonder if you would have that same level of belief.

It's important to remember that faith is grown. It takes time to build trust in the Lord—something we learn from powerful scriptures and personal experiences. Every time we choose to trust God, faith grows. When we lean into Him through prayer, our faith grows. When we give up control and ask Him to intervene, it grows our faith. And in those moments where we're struggling to believe He can and will, let's ask God to increase our faith in Him.

*Father, it helps knowing that even people in the Bible wrestled with
their own belief in You. Thank You for including their stories because
it helps me feel like my grappling isn't a disqualifier. Now I know
I can just ask for an increase! In Jesus' name I pray, amen.*

CHRIST IN YOU

I have been crucified with Christ [in Him I have shared His crucifixion];
it is no longer I who live, but Christ (the Messiah) lives in me; and the life
I now live in the body I live by faith in (by adherence to and reliance on and
complete trust in) the Son of God, Who loved me and gave Himself up for me.
GALATIANS 2:20 AMPC

Think about this: if Christ lives in you, you have access to His supernatural faith. On your own, faith will waver because it's fueled by your humanity—humanity that is weak and flawed by itself. But now, since you have accepted Jesus as your Savior, you have the resource to supercharge your faith. The little bit you brought to the table has been increased by the Lord.

So when you're wrestling with hope that your relationship can get better, ask the Lord for confidence. When you are fighting to embrace the new health diagnosis, believe that God will give you grace for it. When you feel like grief will never end, trust Him for peace to navigate it. It is Christ in you that makes these things possible. He empowers you so you can put your complete trust in Him for anything.

Father, help me live by faith. Give me courage to fully
rely on You for the things I need. And thank You for
the gift of Jesus. In His name I pray, amen.

WHAT WILL THEY SAY ABOUT YOUR FAITH?

*And now the time is fast approaching for my release from this life and
I am ready to be offered as a sacrifice. I have fought an excellent fight.
I have finished my full course and I've kept my heart full of faith.*

2 TIMOTHY 4:6–7 TPT

At the end of your life, what will others say of you? Will they talk about how hard you worked and all you accomplished? Will they talk about how rich you were? Maybe they will reminisce about your beautiful home or the lavish vacations you took with your family. They might note all your community service hours or how they enjoyed your culinary skills. But friend, what will they say of your faith?

You only get one shot at this, and life really is just a breath. This is the time to let your light shine so God is glorified by your words and actions. What better legacy to leave those you love than one of steadfast faith? You get to choose what kind of inheritance you pass on. Let's choose to be women who will be remembered for our excellent fight, for finishing the race set before us, and for having a heart full of faith.

*Father, help me be so full of faith—even imperfect faith—that I will
be able to influence others for You. Let my reputation reflect the
time I invested in our relationship. In Jesus' name I pray, amen.*

SURRENDER YOUR ANXIETY

Surrender your anxiety! Be silent and stop your striving and
you will see that I am God. I am the God above all the nations,
and I will be exalted throughout the whole earth.

PSALM 46:10 TPT

Sometimes we hold tightly to our anxiety because it gives us a false sense of control. We find comfort in trying to figure everything out on our own. We may think being stressed out shows our attention to detail, and therefore tells our loved ones how much we care for them. Being frazzled may give us a sense of pride as it makes us feel important and necessary. It may feed into a victim mentality, giving us plenty to complain about as we collect sympathy. But none of these are good reasons to white knuckle stress as we find ourselves wilting.

The command we read in today's verse is clear: God wants us to give up anxiety. He wants us to stop whining about it—stop trying to fix it—and let Him bring clarity and peace. God is asking you to take a step back and let Him be God. . .and you be you. He is reminding you of His willingness and ability to bring order from the chaos.

●

Father, I hear You loud and clear. Forgive me for trying to play
God with my stress and strife. I am surrendering my anxiety
and choosing to live in peace! In Jesus' name I pray, amen.

FAITH MATTERS

*And so faith, hope, love abide [faith—conviction and
belief respecting man's relation to God and divine things;
hope—joyful and confident expectation of eternal salvation;
love—true affection for God and man, growing out of God's
love for and in us], these three; but the greatest of these is love.*

1 Corinthians 13:13 AMPC

Most of the time, people look at the thirteenth chapter in Corinthians as a discussion about the importance of love. While Paul unpacks this topic beautifully, at the very end he reminds us there are three things the Lord holds dear. Right there, we're told that faith is weighty and matters greatly to the Lord.

The reality is that without it, you cannot be in community with God. It's the glue that holds your relationship together, and it pleases the Lord. It's what you draw on to navigate the choppy waters of life. It's what gives you courage to try again and wisdom to know the next step. It's why you are drawn to read the Bible and pray and can find peace in the midst of chaos. It's a vital part of the trio Paul is talking about. You need all three because they work in powerful combination with one another.

●

*Father, please grow my faith. I'm trying to walk it out daily,
but it's not always pretty. I know You aren't looking for perfection,
but instead purposeful living. In Jesus' name I pray, amen.*

THE POWER THAT BRINGS THE WORLD TO ITS KNEES

Every God-born person conquers the world's ways. The conquering power that brings the world to its knees is our faith. The person who wins out over the world's ways is simply the one who believes Jesus is the Son of God.

1 JOHN 5:4–5 MSG

Sometimes it seems like the world is beating us up. It has a special way of punching us right in the gut and making everything look hopeless. We feel overwhelmed by our struggles and underwhelmed by our motivation, and we worry nothing will change. But that kind of stinkin' thinkin' has no room in the life of a woman of faith.

If you are a child of God—if you've asked Jesus to be your personal Lord and Savior—then you are a force to be reckoned with. You're backed by the God of creation who has made a way for victory through the death of His Son on the cross. It's your belief in Him that gives you strength and might to weather the storms of life. It may be rough at times, but you won't be defeated if you trust God through it. So chin up, buttercup, because your faith enables you to win against anything the world throws your way.

Father, thank You for making a way to find victory in a world bent on trying to destroy. I am choosing to stand in that power today! In Jesus' name I pray, amen.

THE WEAPON OF FAITH

In every battle, take faith as your wrap-around shield,
for it is able to extinguish the blazing arrows
coming at you from the Evil One!
EPHESIANS 6:16 TPT

Friend, your faith is something extraordinarily powerful to wield against the forces of evil. Too often, we feel weak and defenseless as the spiritual battles rage in our lives. We cower in fear and walk away rather than use the armor God has created for us. We exhaust ourselves in our own strength rather than stand strong in His. Let's not do this anymore.

We're told that in every battle that comes our way—in every single battle we must face—there is a weapon at our immediate disposal. Our faith. And when we stand strong and confident, trusting that God is present with us, the enemy's plans are destroyed. Every arrow of hate, insecurity, fear, shame, guilt, and worthlessness is extinguished as we choose to believe who God says we are instead. You are not a wimp. You are not helpless. So grab hold of your shield of faith and stand your ground, mighty warrior.

Father, I confess I feel weak at times. I've never thought of myself as a warrior.
But I know You will give me what I need to defeat the enemy of my soul,
and I know my faith is key in doing so. Please give me courage and confidence
to raise my shield of faith and trust in You. In Jesus' name I pray, amen.

A SAVING FAITH

He said to them, "You are from below; I'm from above. You are from this world; I'm not from this world. This is why I told you that you would die in your sins. If you don't believe that I Am, you will die in your sins." "Who are you?" they asked. Jesus replied, "I'm exactly who I have claimed to be from the beginning."

JOHN 8:23–25 CEB

Jesus laid down some hard truth to a Pharisee in the temple who couldn't wrap his mind around this man claiming to be the Son of God. And because the Pharisee didn't have faith, Jesus clearly explained that he would perish to an eternity separate from God. In his ignorance, he asked, "Who are you?"

Do you have a saving faith in Jesus? Do you know who He is and what He's done to ensure that you can live in heaven with the Father? If not, and if you want to be saved from your sins, repeat this prayer out loud:

Father, I confess I'm a sinner in need of a Savior. I confess I cannot manage this life without You. And I know You're the Way, the Truth, and the Life. Would You be my personal Savior? I acknowledge Jesus as Your Son who paid the price for my sins, and I receive Him into my life and into my heart. Thank You for making a way to an eternity with You! In Jesus' name I pray, amen.

FAITH CAN OPEN A HEART

*Faith opened Noah's heart to receive revelation and warnings from
God about what was coming, even things that had never been seen.
But he stepped out in reverent obedience to God and built an ark that
would save him and his family. By his faith the world was condemned,
but Noah received God's gift of righteousness that comes by believing.*

HEBREWS 11:7 TPT

Faith opened Noah's heart. What a beautiful picture this paints. It's notable, because we know a heart is a tricky thing and can harden from time and trouble. Faith enabled Noah to hear God's warnings about things he couldn't even see yet, as well as obey His instructions to build a massive boat to save his family. And it was because of his faith to do what God asked that the world's ways were proven wrong. Faith is a powerful force fueled by the Holy Spirit.

Where does faith need to open your heart to hear God? Where is He asking you to follow His leading and you're choosing to be stubborn? How is the Lord trying to capture your attention? What next step is He prompting you to take? Make listening for the Lord a daily practice, and obeying a seamless response.

*Father, I don't want to block faith from moving me to follow You.
Give me a willing spirit to hear and obey. In Jesus' name I pray, amen.*

GIVE IT ALL YOU'VE GOT

*Keep your eyes open, hold tight to your convictions,
give it all you've got, be resolute, and love without stopping.*
1 Corinthians 16:13–14 msg

You are not a quitter. Yes, there are times it feels like the best option. There are situations that look hopeless and you want to walk away. There are circumstances where failure seems inevitable. But unless the Lord is telling you to quit, ask Him for the faith to keep moving forward. He will always be there to help you. Without question, you can always count on God.

Need strength for the battle? Ask for it. Need resolve to do the right thing or wisdom to know what's next? Ask. Need clear eyes to see what's happening or the ability to love someone difficult? Ask God to give those abilities to you. Sometimes it's when we get to the end of ourselves—the end of our human solutions and fixes—that we realize we need God. What if instead, we activated our faith at the first sign of trouble? What if we trusted Him for our needs? God is waiting for you to engage His help.

*Father, help me remember that You are the Giver of all good things.
Help me go directly to You first rather than battle myself into exhaustion.
I need Your strength coursing through my veins to give me courage and
confidence to walk through my life well. In Jesus' name I pray, amen.*

YOUR FAITH HEALS

So he threw off his beggars' cloak, jumped up, and made his way
to Jesus. Jesus said to him, "What do you want me to do for you?"
The man replied, "My Master, please, let me see again!" Jesus responded,
"Your faith heals you. Go in peace, with your sight restored." All at once,
the man's eyes opened and he could see again, and he began at
once to follow Jesus, walking down the road with him.

Mark 10:50–52 TPT

Can you even imagine the elation this blind man felt when Jesus healed him in an instant? How many years had he wished for sight? How long had he been craving to see the world around him? Whose face had he wanted to see the very most? When Jesus heard this man's words and saw his belief, the Lord restored his sight instantaneously. His faith made healing possible.

Your story may not be his story, but that doesn't negate the truth that faith unlocks healing. And be it healing physically, emotionally, financially, or some other way, it's your willingness to trust God in your situation that makes it possible. Where do you need healing today? In faith, ask the Lord to help.

Father, give me the kind of faith that believes in Your ability to heal.
Keep me from doubt, and instead build my confidence to have faith
in You no matter what comes my way. In Jesus' name I pray, amen.

YOUR FAITH SHOWS

*It's news I'm most proud to proclaim, this extraordinary Message of
God's powerful plan to rescue everyone who trusts him, starting with
Jews and then right on to everyone else! God's way of putting people
right shows up in the acts of faith, confirming what Scripture has said all
along: "The person in right standing before God by trusting him really lives."*

ROMANS 1:16–17 MSG

When you become a follower of Jesus, it shows. It may not be something
one can see on your face, but faith shows itself to others by how you
act. It's in the way you treat the waitress with kindness when the meal
you ordered is wrong. It's how you choose to forgive someone who
doesn't deserve it. It's revealed in the grace you extend rather than
picking up an offense, letting someone off the hook for hurting your
feelings. It's shown by your selflessness as you help a family in need.
It's in the hours you give toward a needy charity.

Don't misunderstand. Your works don't get you into heaven. It's
by faith alone, believing Jesus is the Son of God. But once you receive
the gift of salvation, your faith is revealed through your actions of love.

*Father, help my actions expose my belief in You. Give me the
spiritual eyes and ears to see the needs of others and respond
in faith as Your hands and feet. In Jesus' name I pray, amen.*

THE BEAUTY OF HUMILITY

Look at the proud; his soul is not straight or right within him,
but the [rigidly] just and the [uncompromisingly] righteous
man shall live by his faith and in his faithfulness.

HABAKKUK 2:4 AMPC

God does not like it when we are prideful. He appreciates a humble heart because it reveals we're not so self-assured that we don't understand our need for God. We can have trust in our abilities because we know they are from the Lord. We can believe in our ability to overcome hardship because we know He will give us strength and endurance. And we can have faith in our decisions because we've asked God for wisdom and discernment. We are trusting Him in us and working through us. Amen?

When we instead think we're epic and awesome on our own, we are sure to fail. There is no room for that kind of prideful mindset as Christians. It's true that God created us with talents and giftings that will take us so far in life. But when we couple those with our faith, they are supercharged. Let's choose to be women who try to live every day honoring God and trusting Him to unpack His will for our life. Let's live by faith.

●

Father, I know You are the reason I can boast because You
are the Giver of all good things. Help me live faithfully,
trusting You to lead me. In Jesus' name I pray, amen.

RIGHT IN THE MIDDLE

I pray that God, the source of all hope, will infuse your lives with
an abundance of joy and peace in the midst of your faith so that
your hope will overflow through the power of the Holy Spirit.

ROMANS 15:13 VOICE

Sometimes it's the middle of a situation that is the messiest. Once the shock has worn off, we find ourselves in the daily grind of walking out the healing journey or facing the ugly consequences. It's grueling. And the middle is usually when we lose hope and want to throw in the towel. Our faith is hanging by a thread.

Be encouraged by today's verse. It shows us that we can pray for God's help when we find ourselves in the messy middle. As we continue to put one foot of faith after the other, taking the next step toward reconciliation, we can ask God to infuse us with abundance. You can ask for joy, peace, and hope. And it's your belief in His ability—be it big or small—that opens the door for the Holy Spirit to flood you with exactly what you need to keep going.

Father, I'm right in the middle of a hard season and in desperate need
of encouragement that things will get better and I will get through it.
Please infuse me with Your hope, joy, and peace. In Jesus' name I pray, amen.

FIGHT OR FLIGHT

Don't run from tests and hardships, brothers and sisters. As difficult as they are, you will ultimately find joy in them; if you embrace them, your faith will blossom under pressure and teach you true patience as you endure. And true patience brought on by endurance will equip you to complete the long journey and cross the finish line— mature, complete, and wanting nothing.

JAMES 1:2–4 VOICE

Yowza. James's call to action seems counterintuitive when life gets hard, doesn't it? When we feel overwhelmed and underwater, running away seems like a viable option. Who really wants to stick it out just to learn the value of patience? Who thinks staying in the middle of the mess will eventually produce joy? Anyone?

But James is sharing some powerful truths that are worthy of a reread. He is offering a change in perspective that will answer the *why* when you're trying to decide how to respond to your tough situation. Because when you find the courage to face it and embrace it, trusting the Lord along the way, your faith will grow deep roots of joy, patience, and endurance. And those roots will keep you securely anchored for the rest of your life.

Father, give me the confidence I need to stand strong in the storms of life. I don't want to give in and miss the gifts that come with staying present in hard times. In Jesus' name I pray, amen.

CREDITED FAITH

He never stopped believing God's promise, for he was made strong in his faith to father a child. And because he was mighty in faith and convinced that God had all the power needed to fulfill his promises, Abraham glorified God! So now you can see why Abraham's faith was credited to his account as righteousness before God.

ROMANS 4:20–22 TPT

Did you know that Abraham was almost one hundred years old when God promised him a son? Even more, Sarah was incapable of getting pregnant. Talk about an unlikely promise! But Abraham believed, nonetheless. He stood in his faith, unwavering even knowing the impossibility of such a thing in the natural. He knew nothing was impossible to God and chose to glorify Him for the power He possessed. In return, the Lord credited his earthly faith to his heavenly account.

What promise has God laid on your heart that feels impossible to you right now? A restored friendship? Finding a spouse? Having kids or raising the ones you have? Paying off the medical bills? Getting past the grief? Speaking your truth? A new job? No matter what the circumstances surrounding it may look like, choose to be like Abraham . . .and believe. That kind of faith will pay dividends in the end.

Father, even when it seems unlikely, I am choosing to trust that You will do what You said You will do! In Jesus' name I pray, amen.

IN ACCORDANCE

For this reason I am telling you, whatever things you ask for in prayer [in accordance with God's will], believe [with confident trust] that you have received them, and they will be given to you.

MARK 11:24 AMP

Sometimes we read this verse and think God is a genie in a bottle, and we get three (or more) wishes. We interpret it as whatever we ask for—if we really want it—it will be ours. But that is not reality. No loving God would give us anything and everything we wanted. If He did, why would we need to trust Him?

Instead, what we need to count on is that God will always respond with what is best for us. While He's always listening to our requests and loves that we're big dreamers, sometimes what we want isn't in His plan. It may carry consequences too big to shoulder. Or it may be the wrong timing. So when you ask God for something, end each request with a reminder that you will always trust His will and His timing. That way, your faith is secured in God Himself and not His willingness or ability to give you what you want.

Father, thank You for the freedom to ask You for anything. And thank You for loving me enough for that answer to sometimes be. . .no. Help me trust Your response over what I think is best for me. In Jesus' name I pray, amen.

HOW TO FIGHT
THE GOOD FIGHT

*Timothy, don't let this happen to you—run away from these
things! You are a man of God. Your quest is for justice, godliness,
faithfulness, love, perseverance, and gentleness. Fight the good
fight of the faith! Cling to the eternal life you were called to
when you confessed the good confession before witnesses.*
1 TIMOTHY 6:11–12 VOICE

Just as Paul was urging Timothy to stay true to his faith in God, let his
words be an encouragement to you too. So many things out there are
designed to destroy our walk with Him. From the things we watch and
read, to the attitudes and prejudices we carry, to our thought life and
actions, the world never gives us a break.

Our job—and it's a big one—is to live in the right way. We are to
pursue and serve the Lord with our lives. We're to trust Him to grow
the fruit of the Spirit in us so we can love those around us. And we
are to trust God, building our faith in His will and ways every day.
These are the ways we fight the good fight, friend! This is how we
point others to God in heaven!

*Father, help me keep my eyes on You. Let me never give up
pursuing Your will in my life. And bless me with the desire
to love You with all my heart. In Jesus' name I pray, amen.*

THE PURSUIT OF GREAT FAITH

Then Jesus answered her, "Woman, your faith [your personal trust and confidence in My power] is great; it will be done for you as you wish." And her daughter was healed from that moment.

MATTHEW 15:28 AMP

What would it take for your faith to be great? Maybe right now, your faith is as small as a mustard seed. Maybe you are still trying to figure out the whole God thing, or you've lost your faith somewhere along the way and are struggling to get it back. Regardless of the why, what do you need to make it great?

Faith is a choice. It's a decision to believe in a God we cannot see. It's allowing your need for control to dim as your hope in Him brightens. And honestly, faith is something God grows in us. We simply cannot do it without Him. So when you need strength for that hard conversation or grace for someone who hurt your feelings, when you need wisdom to take the right step or peace to calm your nerves, when you need endurance for the process and courage for prognosis, ask God for it. And every time you see Him come through, you'll be on your way to a great faith.

●

Father, I know the size of my faith doesn't matter but instead the willingness to have it. Thank You for growing it in me when I ask. I love You! In Jesus' name I pray, amen.

CONSISTENT FAITH

And Jesus, replying, said to them,
Have faith in God [constantly].
MARK 11:22 AMPC

This means when the doctor's diagnosis scares you to death, you trust God through the process. When your child is making decisions that are hurtful, you have hope in His promises. When your spouse's secrets come to light and divorce is imminent, the Lord becomes your refuge. When you feel persecuted for speaking your heart to someone, you cling to God for comfort. And when you are so lonely and feel unloved, you choose to believe who God says you are.

At the end of the day, all you really have is the Lord. You may have a great support system that loves you dearly, but they are not your savior. You might have a full calendar to keep your mind occupied, but that can't heal your heart. Remember that you have God, and He is always in your corner. When you choose to constantly trust Him with anything and everything, you will have all you need to walk out this life well.

Father, it's hard to have constant faith because there are many things that can shake it loose. Sometimes I feel overwhelmed with my life, and I try to fix it myself. I rely on me. And it's later that I remember You. Forgive me for that and help me run to You first. In Jesus' name I pray, amen.

HIS PATH THROUGH
THE VALLEY

Lord, even when your path takes me through the valley of deepest darkness,
fear will never conquer me, for you already have! You remain close to me and
lead me through it all the way. Your authority is my strength and my peace. The
comfort of your love takes away my fear. I'll never be lonely, for you are near.

PSALM 23:4 TPT

God loves you. He cares so much for your heart. And He is focused on growing you into the woman He intended for you to be. Sometimes the only way to grow your faith is to allow hardship into your life. That isn't because God is mean. It's because He knows it's sometimes the best way for us to learn. Think about it. What's the incentive to change and grow when life is good? There is none.

But when we're walking through the valley—trusting the Lord to lead and sustain—our heart is desperate for His comfort. We surrender to His plan, knowing it's our only hope. We crave His shelter and protection. And we follow where He leads because we know He will safely get us through to the other side.

Father, grow my faith in the valleys. Teach me to put my trust
in You, knowing You'll never leave me to fend for myself. Give me
courage to surrender my fears to You in exchange for comfort.
Thank You for being with me. In Jesus' name I pray, amen.

NEVER BE ASHAMED

I refuse to be ashamed of sharing the wonderful message
of God's liberating power unleashed in us through Christ!
For I am thrilled to preach that everyone who believes is
saved—the Jew first, and then people everywhere!

ROMANS 1:16 TPT

Especially in these days, sharing our faith is often met with negativity. People may find us simple for just believing in Jesus, certain their state of enlightenment makes more sense. Many think the Bible is a book full of made-up stories. They call it irrelevant and unnecessary. And they consider it foolish to put our trust in anything or anyone we cannot see. This kind of mentality is so prevalent today, and it's often the reason we keep our mouths shut. We are scared to promote Jesus. We're worried about being shamed for believing. And so rather than live our faith out loud, we choose to tuck it in and stay quiet.

Friend, choose to be a light! If the things we say don't point others to the Lord, how will they hear? If the way we live doesn't reveal His love, who misses out? Go ahead and put yourself out there. You don't have to picket with signs or preach with a megaphone. Just let your words and actions reflect the faith you have in God.

Father, give me the courage to be bold for You! Help me shine
You into the world in a powerful way! In Jesus' name I pray, amen.

GENUINE FAITH

Pure gold put in the fire comes out of it proved pure; genuine faith put through this suffering comes out proved genuine. When Jesus wraps this all up, it's your faith, not your gold, that God will have on display as evidence of his victory.

1 Peter 1:7 msg

When you have come through the storm still praising the Lord, your faith is proven genuine. In those seasons where most would have walked away from God in anger, but you stayed in a position of trust, your faith is authenticated. When you get sucker punched in the gut by life but continue to believe in the promises of God, your faith proves victorious. And the Lord is pleased!

The Bible tells us we will face many trials along the way but to let our faith be the reminder that God is with us. That He is trustworthy and will be there every step of the way. It takes guts and grit to continue to trust Him when we want to freak out. It's not easy to give up control and activate our faith. But when we do, God will bless us for staying true to His promises.

Father, I want my faith to be proven genuine. I want others to see You in how I choose to live my life. I want Your name glorified in my responses. Please strengthen my faith every day so I can delight Your heart. In Jesus' name I pray, amen.

OPPORTUNITY TO TRUST MORE

We all experience times of testing, which is normal for every human being. But God will be faithful to you. He will screen and filter the severity, nature, and timing of every test or trial you face so that you can bear it. And each test is an opportunity to trust him more, for along with every trial God has provided for you a way of escape that will bring you out of it victoriously.

1 CORINTHIANS 10:13 TPT

What an amazing God we serve! His faithfulness to us is remarkable, and unmatched by anyone else. Not only does He screen and filter every test and trial that comes our way, but He provides an escape button, so we don't get snagged. He makes sure there's a way for us to be victorious through our struggle. And when we choose to activate our faith, God not only recognizes our choice to trust Him, but He also blesses it. Even more, the Lord uses those times to deepen our relationship.

It's so important that we realize we aren't alone when temptation hits. It's not about our level of willpower. It's not about our resolve. There is no magical formula we can access for a win. It's all about calling on God for help.

Father, You're so awesome! Thank You for making a way out when I feel trapped in a trial or test. Remind me to trust You. In Jesus' name I pray, amen.

THE PRODUCER

*The Holy Spirit produces a different kind of fruit: unconditional love,
joy, peace, patience, kindheartedness, goodness, faithfulness, gentleness,
and self-control. You won't find any law opposed to fruit like this.*
GALATIANS 5:22–23 VOICE

Did you notice who the producer is in today's verse? It's the Holy Spirit alone. We often miss this, deciding that growing in our faith, love, and self-control is all about us. We think finding peace and joy is our job. We believe in fighting our way to patience. We put the burden of maturity on our own shoulders. In our mind, the pressure is heavy to be a better Christian, and so we push and push to meet certain standards.

But maybe our response should instead be asking the Holy Spirit to lead this effort. Maybe we should surrender our control and ask for Him to take over. The truth is that these fruits need divine intervention to develop. We simply don't have the skill or power to mature them ourselves. And when we put our faith in the Holy Spirit, He will ripen in accordance with God's will.

*Father, help me trust You through the process of maturing the gifts of the
Spirit in my life. Give me the ability to relinquish control. Teach me how to
surrender my desires and timing to You. And please increase my faith as
I allow the Spirit to produce these in me. In Jesus' name I pray, amen.*

A BEAUTIFUL FUTURE

*"For I know the plans I have for you," says the Eternal, "plans
for peace, not evil, to give you a future and hope—never forget that.
At that time, you will call out for Me, and I will hear. You will pray,
and I will listen. You will look for Me intently, and you will find Me."*
JEREMIAH 29:11–13 VOICE

Sometimes it takes all we have to believe God has good and hopeful plans for our future. We look at the mess of our current situation and lose hope that this promise is for us. We reflect on our choppy past and struggle to see anything positive. We look at the trajectory of our life going forward and feel discouraged. But we forget that our Father knows every plan He designed for us.

Every morning welcome the Lord into the details of your day. Ask for an increase in faith to hear and see Him. Invite God into your hopelessness and fear and share your deepest concerns. Tell Him you need encouragement to know He hasn't forgotten you. And maybe ask God to remind you of the value you hold in His eyes. We all need reassurance that He is trustworthy, and that He has plans for our beautiful future.

*Father, help me trust You with what's ahead, knowing
Your heart for me is always good. Give me the confidence
to walk into my future boldly. In Jesus' name I pray, amen.*

FAITH SET UP

Just then a woman who had hemorrhaged for twelve years slipped in
from behind and lightly touched his robe. She was thinking to herself,
"If I can just put a finger on his robe, I'll get well." Jesus turned—caught
her at it. Then he reassured her: "Courage, daughter. You took a risk
of faith, and now you're well." The woman was well from then on.
MATTHEW 9:20–22 MSG

Have you ever been desperate for the healing only God can provide? Have you been so undone that you knew He was your only hope? Have you ever been at the end of yourself and faith in the Lord was all you had left? You're not alone, friend. And what a gift that God included this woman's story in the Bible. He knew we'd need a reminder of what our faith initiates.

She had exhausted her finances and her medical options. For her, Jesus was the last hope. She mustered her faith and made her way through the crowd, touching only the hem of His robe but believing it was enough. And right then and there, she was healed. Her faith set her up for healing. Choose to believe in His power and watch what happens.

Father, I want that kind of faith. I want to believe in Your power
so deeply and without question. Help me risk it all to trust that
You will come through for me. In Jesus' name I pray, amen.

JUDGING THE FAITH OF OTHERS

Welcome with open arms fellow believers who don't see things the way you do. And don't jump all over them every time they do or say something you don't agree with—even when it seems that they are strong on opinions but weak in the faith department. Remember, they have their own history to deal with. Treat them gently.

ROMANS 14:1 MSG

We all have our own faith journey to work out. Each of us will need to determine what kind of relationship we'll have with the Lord. There's no cookie-cutter path that fits us all. And while some will have deep roots of faith with mature wisdom and discernment, others will not. Through those different lenses, we will inevitably disagree and have opposing ideas on certain things. Today's verse is a great reminder to treat one another with kindness as well as give the necessary space to be ourselves.

Let's choose to be women who don't sit in judgment of another's faith. Let's not point to it as why—in our opinion—they did or did not handle a situation correctly. We're not the authority on faith. That's between them and God. Instead, let's decide to love everyone right where they are. Isn't that what God asks of us anyway?

Father, give me grace for others. Give me a heart to love without condemnation, unconcerned about where someone is in their faith journey. In Jesus' name I pray, amen.

GOD OF THE IMPOSSIBLE

Because of faith also Sarah herself received physical power to conceive a child, even when she was long past the age for it, because she considered [God] Who had given her the promise to be reliable and trustworthy and true to His word.

HEBREWS 11:11 AMPC

Be encouraged by Sarah's story! She was years past menopause, physically unable to conceive and carry a child—the child God promised Abraham. It was literally impossible. Undoable. Inconceivable. In the natural, there was no way this old woman could make this happen. Aging had taken its toll and closed the door to pregnancy long ago. It simply could not happen. But Sarah—in a decision of faith—believed God.

There is nothing that bars the Lord from doing His will. He isn't imprisoned by any constraint. God is above all rules or regulations. So friend, when you look at your situation and see a closed door, He never does. When your circumstance is impossible to you, it most certainly is not to God. Let today's scripture encourage you to step out in faith and believe Him. Believe that He is a God of can-dos.

Father, I confess that I doubt You sometimes. Thank You for being patient with my battle of believing. Would You help my faith and trust in You grow so I know deep in my DNA that You are the God of the impossible? In Jesus' name I pray, amen.

BELIEVE DEEP

*So if you believe deep in your heart that God raised Jesus from
the pit of death and if you voice your allegiance by confessing the
truth that "Jesus is Lord," then you will be saved! Belief begins
in the heart and leads to a life that's right with God; confession
departs from our lips and brings eternal salvation.*

Romans 10:9–10 voice

Paul is setting us straight by calling us deeper in our belief. It's one thing to say we believe in something, but it's completely different when we allow it to sink into our DNA. And there's a distinction between talking about something you believe in and confessing with confidence. It's the difference between believing with your head and knowing deep in your heart. The verse tells us that faith begins in the heart, and it's from there we live. That's how we are able to walk every day in a right relationship with God. If our faith isn't rooted deep, the storms of life will rock it every time.

How deep is your faith right now? What keeps you from trusting more? Take time today to unpack your relationship with the Lord. Ask Him to open your eyes to barriers that might be blocking deeper faith. Tell Him your fears and concerns. And ask Him to open your heart to a greater level of faith.

*Father, I want more of You. I want more of us.
Please deepen my faith. In Jesus' name I pray, amen.*

EVEN WITHOUT SEEING

You love him passionately although you did not see him, but through believing in him you are saturated with an ecstatic joy, indescribably sublime and immersed in glory. For you are reaping the harvest of your faith—the full salvation promised you—your souls' victory!

1 PETER 1:8–9 TPT

It is possible to love the Lord without ever seeing Him with our eyes or hearing His voice with our ears. The definition of faith in Jesus is having complete trust in Him even though you cannot see Him this side of heaven. It's a choice to believe in His existence without any visual or audible confirmation while in this world. And sometimes. . .it's so hard to do.

When we are angry, we want to sit and process with someone. When we're hurting, we want to hear validation and empathy. When we're confused, we want to talk through what to do next. But it's our faith that allows the Lord to meet all those needs for us. Through His Word, time in prayer, and godly advice from those we trust, we can have a deeply rooted relationship with God—a relationship so secure that we'll find joy as we journey through the junk of life on our way to eternity with Him.

Father, increase my faith. Teach me to be deeply rooted in my belief so I can walk through life in a right relationship with You. In Jesus' name I pray, amen.

HE WILL FULLY SATISFY

I am convinced that my God will fully satisfy every need you have,
for I have seen the abundant riches of glory revealed to me through
the Anointed One, Jesus Christ! And God our Father will receive all the
glory and the honor throughout the eternity of eternities! Amen!

PHILIPPIANS 4:19–20 TPT

What are your needs right now, today? Maybe you need a job so you can pay off the rising stack of bills. Maybe you need a friend who will break the loneliness you're experiencing. Maybe you want to be married and have a happily ever after, or you want kids to fill the rooms in your home. Maybe you need grace for that one person who is driving you nuts, or maybe you need grace given to you. Maybe you need hope that things will get better.

Faith is how we navigate all these needs and wants. This is where we believe He will either fully satisfy those exact needs just how we've asked or find peace as He redirects us according to His will. Faith is how we find contentment either way. Faith is trust on steroids, and when we activate our faith, we surrender control and allow the Lord to satisfy us in His timing and His ways.

Father, I trust You to meet my needs however
You see fit! I know You always have my best
in mind. In Jesus' name I pray, amen.

LEAN ON HIM

*Commit your way to the Lord [roll and repose each care of your
load on Him]; trust (lean on, rely on, and be confident) also in Him
and He will bring it to pass. And He will make your uprightness and
right standing with God go forth as the light, and your justice
and right as [the shining sun of] the noonday.*

PSALM 37:5-6 AMPC

God wants you to lean on Him when you're feeling weak. He wants every single worry or insecurity off your shoulders and onto His. When you are hopeless, He wants you to rely on Him for an increase. Anytime you are overwhelmed, the Lord wants your confidence in Him to grow deep roots. He is after your heart and wants you to find rest knowing He will take care of everything weighing you down right now.

Make time today for a personal inventory of the heavy things in your life. Where are you feeling overloaded? Where are you offended? Who is causing you stress and strife? Where are you struggling with confidence or courage? Why are you anxious? These are the exact things the Lord wants you to trust Him with. Let Him be the soft landing you lean into.

*Father, I lay my worries and fears at Your feet and ask for
a sense of Your comfort. Help me find rest in You. And give me the
faith necessary to lean on You every time. In Jesus' name I pray, amen.*

TRUST HIS TIMING

*So be content with who you are, and don't put on
airs. God's strong hand is on you; he'll promote you at the
right time. Live carefree before God; he is most careful with you.*

1 PETER 5:6–7 MSG

One of the hardest things to do is trust God's timing. Why? Because it never seems to match ours. Amen? What we may think qualifies for an emergency response may not look the same to the Lord. In our desperation, we might activate our faith and cry out for help, healing, and hope. But God may be waiting for things to fall into place before He responds. And while it may look and feel like our prayers are bouncing off the ceiling, the Lord is busy at work on our behalf.

It's important we trust God's timing. It's a choice we have to make every day. And it's vital for our head and heart to know that He is always active in our life. In faith we have to remember He loves us with an everlasting and unchanging love. And when we settle these truths in our spirit, we will have peace.

*Father, help me remember that Your heart for me is always good
and that You will not leave me to figure things out on my own. I am
desperate for Your love, guidance, and provision, so help remove any
barrier that blocks that truth from my heart. In Jesus' name I pray, amen.*

HE'LL TAKE YOUR SIDE

Take my side, God—I'm getting kicked around, stomped on every day.
Not a day goes by but somebody beats me up; they make it their duty
to beat me up. When I get really afraid I come to you in trust. I'm proud
to praise God; fearless now, I trust in God. What can mere mortals do?

PSALM 56:1-4 MSG

Ever feel like the world is beating you up? Ever feel like everyone is against you, and they're rooting for your demise? In self-loathing, have you labeled yourself a quitter? A failure? A disappointment? Does it seem as if you're always falling short of the expectations of others? Deep breath, friend. The truth is, there is no shortage of hard things, hateful people, and hurtful situations. It could be a relationship that has gone south, a financial strain that feels unfixable, or a diagnosis that will dramatically change how you live your life. Life is difficult at best.

But never forget that because of your faith in Jesus, you have an unshakable ally. He will never walk away from you. You can't be too needy. And your messy will never be *too* messy. And while your choices often carry inescapable consequences, that doesn't mean the Lord is done with you. Instead, it means He will walk with you through it— from beginning to end.

Father, what a comfort to know You will always
have my back. Thank You! In Jesus' name I pray, amen.

THE TENDENCY TO BACK AWAY

There is no fear in love [dread does not exist]. But perfect (complete, full-grown) love drives out fear, because fear involves [the expectation of divine] punishment, so the one who is afraid [of God's judgment] is not perfected in love [has not grown into a sufficient understanding of God's love].

1 JOHN 4:18 AMP

Are you afraid of God? Do you worry you've made Him mad because of something you said or did? Maybe you feel guilty or ashamed by how you behaved in a situation. Maybe you feel like you've let God down one too many times. Maybe you feel like a liability or believe that His love for someone like you has limits. . .and you've reached them.

Here's the problem with that train of thought: When we believe these things, it keeps us from exercising our faith. We don't feel like we can ask for His help. We don't feel we have the right to trust He will provide. And we back away from a God who loves us unconditionally. The truth is that fear isn't from the Lord. We should never be afraid of Him. Through the Holy Spirit we are convicted but not condemned. Be careful that nothing ever encourages your faith to wither.

Father, help me remember that I am fully and completely loved by You, and that Your heart for me is always good! In Jesus' name I pray, amen.

HOW MUCH LONGER?

I'm hurting, Lord—will you forget me forever? How much longer, Lord?
Will you look the other way when I'm in need? How much longer must I
cling to this constant grief? I've endured this shaking of my soul. So how
much longer will my enemy have the upper hand? It's been long enough!
PSALM 13:1–2 TPT

Chances are you've felt this way too. Can you think back to a time you were at the end of your rope, barely hanging on? Remember when you were anxiously awaiting breakthrough? Life has a special way of beating us up, doesn't it? And there are times it feels like everything is hitting us at the same time. Maybe you're even struggling with that right now.

In today's verse, the psalmist is desperate for relief—ready for a break—but here's what is so cool. Here is your gold nugget: he knows that God is the answer. It's his faith that reminds him that he needs the Lord. Take this nugget with you from today forward. The next time you find yourself in a hard place, activate your faith and cry out to God for intervention.

Father, I confess I don't like waiting. When I am hurting, I want relief right away.
Help me find peace in knowing that You hear my cries and are active in my
situation, even if I can't see it in the moment. In Jesus' name I pray, amen.

PEACE FOR TRUSTING

You will keep the peace, a perfect peace, for all who trust in You, for those who dedicate their hearts and minds to You. So trust in the Eternal One forever, for He is like a great Rock—strong, stable, trustworthy, and lasting.

Isaiah 26:3–4 VOICE

There is a beautiful exchange that takes place when you choose to trust God. It's a divine deposit that helps sustain you in your unsettling moments. Without fail, the Lord makes a promise to replace those emotions that keep you stirred up with peace. He recognizes the faith it takes to trust Him instead of trying to control everyone and everything. He sees the dedication you're showing to believing God's sovereignty. And He rewards you for it.

The Lord will never leave you hopeless or helpless when you need Him. God is a stabilizing force when the ground under you begins to shake with worry or fear. He is faithful to fulfill every promise and stand by you through every messy moment. Even more, God's unwavering love for you is forever and for always. Your faith in Him unlocks endless gifts and blessings. He is always ready and able to help.

Father, I crave peace in my life. Things are so crazy right now, and I'm scared they'll never settle down. I'm discouraged and frustrated. What a relief to know that You will reward my trust in You with peace for me. In Jesus' name I pray, amen.

POWERFUL AND PROUD

Surely those who trust the Eternal—who don't trust in proud,
powerful people or in people who care little for reality, chasing false
gods—surely they are happy, as I have become. You have done so many
wonderful things, had so many tender thoughts toward us, Eternal my
God, that go on and on, ever increasing. Who can compare with You?
PSALM 40:4–5 VOICE

It's so easy for us to blindly trust those we see as powerful people. Whether it's someone we admire in Hollywood or some other icon that lives in the spotlight, too often we become enamored with their opinions or ideas and subscribe. We put our faith in their prescriptions for living and loving, and we come up empty.

But God wants our full trust to be in Him. He isn't a trend that will change with the season or a weak god that will falter when pressed. Instead, the Lord has done amazing things for you. Check His track record in your life. Look at the ways He has saved you, healed you, provided for you, and proved Himself faithful time and time again. He is the only powerful One you can fully trust!

Father, take my eyes off any false god that has caught my attention.
Reveal to me the wrong places I am putting my trust. Help me focus
on You alone. You are the power in my life! In Jesus' name I pray, amen.

YOUR SAFE HOUSE

God's a safe-house for the battered, a sanctuary during bad times.
The moment you arrive, you relax; you're never sorry you knocked.
PSALM 9:9–10 MSG

Your faith is the key to the safe house. When your marriage is falling apart. . .when your health is failing. . .your hope is gone. . .your relationship is crumbling. . .your finances are dwindling. . .your joy is drained and your heart is hurting. . .your insecurity is through the roof and fear overwhelms. . .you can't see the right path. . .run into the arms of God. He is your safe house during the bad times life brings your way.

There is nothing He cannot fix—no issues He cannot overcome for you. No one has God's ability to restore beauty from the ashes of your circumstances. And it's your faith in Him that unleashes His awesomeness in your situation. Your family and friends may adore you and have the very best intentions, but they aren't your savior. They may provide a safe space as best as they can, but they are unable to walk with you like the Lord. There is no substitute.

Father, thank You for being a safe house for the weary—for me.
So often, I want to give up and walk away, but I keep coming
back to You. Give me the courage to knock on Your door during
the hard moments life brings. In Jesus' name I pray, amen.

SATURATED

*Don't be pulled in different directions or worried about a thing.
Be saturated in prayer throughout each day, offering your faith-filled
requests before God with overflowing gratitude. Tell him every detail of
your life, then God's wonderful peace that transcends human understanding,
will make the answers known to you through Jesus Christ.*

<small>Philippians 4:6-7 TPT</small>

This is faith in action. It's a call to put all your eggs in one basket, a challenge to focus your worries in one direction for help and healing. It is choosing to believe God over everything else. So instead of relying on your friends and family, instead of relying on your instincts or wisdom, instead of relying on things taught in self-help books, you saturate yourself in prayers of hope to the Lord. And you sprinkle them with gratitude for what He will do.

Let God be your safe place to purge every fear and frustration. Give Him the gory details of the situation. Gossip away as you unpack the pain in your heart. Empty yourself of every disappointing moment and unmet expectation. Let it all out as you drench your broken heart in His presence through prayer, and then revel in the unmatched peace that will follow.

*Father, it's easy to be pulled in different directions when I'm upset
because I'm desperately looking for something or someone to
help me feel better. Forgive me for not coming to You first. Help me
remember that You're always available! In Jesus' name I pray, amen.*

SO MUCH BETTER

*Lord, it is so much better to trust in you to save me than to put
my confidence in someone else. Yes, it is so much better to trust
in the Lord to save me than to put my confidence in celebrities.*

PSALM 118:8–9 TPT

Who do you put your faith in? Maybe it's your husband or boyfriend, your parents, grandparents, or some other family member. Maybe you put your trust in a certain political party or activist group, buying into their promises for change. It could be a preacher or author. Maybe it's a certain news network or social media platform. It may even be a Hollywood celebrity, reality television personality, or music mogul. Be careful, friend. None of these carry the same weight as the Lord.

The psalmist has the right perspective. He understands who is worthy of our trust and who is not. It doesn't mean these are bad people; it just means they are limited by their humanity. They can only do so much. As much as they may try to be a voice of reason, they are flawed just like we are. And when we place our faith in them and their words, we will eventually be let down. It's inevitable. Let's agree with the psalmist and believe that God is so much better than anything the world has to offer.

*Father, You are worthy of my trust and confidence.
You alone are completely faithful. In Jesus' name I pray, amen.*

FIX YOUR ATTENTION ON GOD

So here's what I want you to do, God helping you: Take your everyday, ordinary life—your sleeping, eating, going-to-work, and walking-around life—and place it before God as an offering. Embracing what God does for you is the best thing you can do for him. Don't become so well-adjusted to your culture that you fit into it without even thinking. Instead, fix your attention on God. You'll be changed from the inside out. Readily recognize what he wants from you, and quickly respond to it. Unlike the culture around you, always dragging you down to its level of immaturity, God brings the best out of you, develops well-formed maturity in you.

Romans 12:1–2 msg

Living a faith-filled life can be boiled down to one intentional focus: *fixing your attention on God*. If you allow that to be your mission statement—the driving force for how you live your life—you will be transformed in the most beautiful ways. It will allow God to bring out the very best in you, maturing your faith into something powerful. And the only way we can truly walk this out every day is with the Lord's help. It's something we'll need to ask for. Be the kind of woman who pursues righteous living and faithful obedience.

Father, help me fix my attention on You every single day so I can deepen my faith. You're my focus. In Jesus' name I pray, amen.

DEEPLY ROOTED

Happy are those who trust in the Lord, who rely on the Lord. They will be like trees planted by the streams, whose roots reach down to the water. They won't fear drought when it comes; their leaves will remain green. They won't be stressed in the time of drought or fail to bear fruit.

JEREMIAH 17:7–8 CEB

Do you ever just want to be happy? With so much stress and strife weighing us down, our pursuit of happy seems to elude us no matter what we do. We try all the tricks of the trade, like eating right, exercising regularly, practicing soothing meditation, attending social gatherings, and speaking affirmations to ourselves in a mirror. But they fall short and we're left feeling blah. But there is a way to find happiness that's scripturally based. Did you catch it in today's reading?

If you surrender control and trust the Lord instead, you will find happiness. Your roots of faith will go down so deep that nothing will sway you. Happiness and joy cannot be stolen because they're firmly planted in your heart. Be it in a valley or on a mountaintop, in abundance or in lacking, you won't be on an emotional roller coaster. It's God's hand through your faith that will keep you steady.

Father, help me trust in You above all else. Grow my roots of faith deep in the soil of Your goodness! In Jesus' name I pray, amen.

CHOOSING NOT TO FEAR

He will not fear bad news; his heart is steadfast,
trusting [confidently relying on and believing] in the LORD.
PSALM 112:7 AMP

Sometimes we get news that knocks us to our knees. It punches us right in the gut, and we're left terrified for what's next. Our anxiety shoots through the roof, our heart starts to race, we feel sick to our stomach, we begin to sweat, and we get scared. What a horrible feeling. The truth is that fear is a big deal, isn't it? It has the ability to stir us up into tears or paralyze us from moving forward. It can make our brain fuzzy as we struggle to make decisions. How do you respond when bad news comes your way?

What if you decided to stop fear in its tracks by going to God immediately? What if instead of going down that path again this time, you chose to trust the Lord's sovereignty and activate your faith, believing that God is always working for your good? What if you asked Him for peace to calm your anxious fear and the courage necessary to trust rather than fear?

Father, give me the kind of faith it takes to choose faith over fear.
When bad news knocks me down, would You give me the courage
to get back up as I trust Your plan? In Jesus' name I pray, amen.

WAITING IN FAITH

But those who wait for the LORD [who expect, look for, and hope in Him]
will gain new strength and renew their power; they will lift up their
wings [and rise up close to God] like eagles [rising toward the sun];
they will run and not become weary, they will walk and not grow tired.
ISAIAH 40:31 AMP

In a world that preaches go, go, go. . .it's hard to find the wherewithal to just take a breath and rest. All you have to do is look at our calendars to see how jam-packed our lives have become. Does anyone have lazy days anymore? Honestly, even if we made space for one here and there, we'd feel guilty for it. We'd worry we weren't productive enough. Somewhere along the way we began to connect our busy schedules to our sense of worth. The busier, the more important.

But God knows the value of waiting. And when we choose to wait for His plan to unfold before jumping into action, there's an award. He incentivizes us to trust. God rewards our faith. And when we allow the Lord space to work in our situation, we receive new strength, renewed power, and unmatched endurance for what's ahead.

Father, give me wisdom to wait on You. Help me see the value in
trusting Your timing in all things. I'm a doer, and so I'll need You to
gently remind me to simply wait in faith. In Jesus' name I pray, amen.

TRUSTING HIM OVER THE WORLD

See those people polishing their chariots, and those others grooming their horses? But we're making garlands for GOD our God. The chariots will rust, those horses pull up lame—and we'll be on our feet, standing tall.

PSALM 20:7-8 MSG

It's so dangerous to put your trust in the things of this world. While its offerings may look like a good option at times, and its promises may be made in spades, the reality is that nothing earthly can deliver without fail. Your friends may have the best intentions to come through for you. Your family may guarantee their loyalty and sacrifice. And you may believe the remedies and solutions many say are time tested and fail-proof. But they will all let you down at one point or another. Nothing here is certain.

Anchor your faith to the Lord. Let Him be what you hold on to when life throws a curve ball. God is always dependable and trustworthy and will never fail you. He is faithful every day and in every way. And when you believe His promises to save and heal, you won't be let down.

Father, help me remember the world has nothing reliable for me to hold on to. Give me the right perspective so I don't put my hope in things that cannot deliver. I want to trust You over the world. I want my faith to rest in You alone. In Jesus' name I pray, amen.

FIXING YOUR HEART ON HIS PROMISES

Keep trusting in the Lord and do what is right in his eyes. Fix your heart on the promises of God and you will be secure, feasting on his faithfulness. Make God the utmost delight and pleasure of your life, and he will provide for you what you desire the most.

PSALM 37:3-4 TPT

Today's verse might be an easy read, but it takes real grit to walk this out. Living in this way is a deliberate choice that often feels counterintuitive. But activating your faith like this is essential to finding peace in a whack-a-doo world.

The challenge is to grab onto God's promises and never let go. Fixing your heart on Him requires you to push out the negative thoughts of hopelessness and instead choose to believe the Lord no matter what. It compels you to hold fast to your faith—even faith the size of a mustard seed—when everyone and everything around you suggest you don't. It is surrendering the tendency to control the outcome and remember all that God has told you. But when you do, you will feel a sense of security unmatched by anything else.

●

Father, it's easy to live for myself and do what I want. But I'm now challenged to refocus my heart on You, trying to live out my faith with purpose and passion. Help me change my gaze to rest on Your faithfulness rather than my selfishness. In Jesus' name I pray, amen.

THE POWER OF WHEN

You are my strength and my shield from every danger. When I fully
trust in you, help is on the way. I jump for joy and burst forth with
ecstatic, passionate praise! I will sing songs of what you mean to me!
You will be the inner strength of all your people, the mighty protector
of all, the saving strength for all your anointed ones.

PSALM 28:7–8 TPT

Notice the word *when* in the second sentence of today's scripture. That is a strong indication that we have to participate in what's next. It's telling us that before the promise is kept, we have a role to play. There is something important on our end that triggers the Lord's blessing. Just as in any relationship, it takes two to tango. Amen?

God promises to bring help when you put your whole faith in Him. It's not that He needs you to encourage Him to intervene. You don't have to persuade your heavenly Father to be involved in your life. Instead, it's that He needs you to be surrendered and watching for His hand in your situation.

Father, I recognize that You are my Strength and Shield. I understand my
need for You in my life. But sometimes I need help putting all my faith in
someone other than myself. Give me courage to surrender control as I
wait for You to fulfill every promise. In Jesus' name I pray, amen.

FAITH SUPPORTED

Meanwhile, the moment we get tired in the waiting, God's Spirit is right alongside helping us along. If we don't know how or what to pray, it doesn't matter. He does our praying in and for us, making prayer out of our wordless sighs, our aching groans. He knows us far better than we know ourselves, knows our pregnant condition, and keeps us present before God. That's why we can be so sure that every detail in our lives of love for God is worked into something good.

Romans 8:26–28 MSG

The Holy Spirit is pretty amazing. He is what makes our faith and trust in God grow and flourish. When we feel weary, He is there. When we want to give up, the Holy Spirit helps us along. And when we don't even have the words to pray or don't know what to ask for, it's the Spirit who intercedes on our behalf to the Father. Because He knows us far better than we know ourselves, He has unique insight into our needs.

The truth is that your faith is supported—always has been and always will be. Consider it a group effort with heaven. And no matter the size of your faith, the Holy Spirit makes up the difference. Let this truth seep into the nooks and crannies of your heart when you feel like your faith isn't good enough.

Father, thank You for the Holy Spirit being active in my life! In Jesus' name I pray, amen.

THE PIT OF HUMAN OPINION

The fear of human opinion disables;
trusting in God protects you from that.
PROVERBS 29:25 MSG

There are few things more dangerous than worrying about what others think of you. When that becomes your focus, that's where you place your faith. You decide if so-and-so approves of your choices, then you're doing a good job. If they give you a thumbs-up for your parenting, then you must be on the right track. If you receive accolades for how you handled the hardship, it must mean you're a rock star. At the core, you're allowing public opinion to become your gauge for worthiness. But friend, these are not the ones you need to impress.

When you instead put God first in your life, concerned more with living a righteous life than pleasing others, your faith acts as a shield of protection from worldly opinions. It takes away the sting of letting others down. It removes any power they may have over your decisions. And it sets right your priorities. Wanting to live in life-giving community with others is noble, but it can't be the hill you die on. The One who died on that hill in Calvary is the only One worthy of your faith.

Father, help me steer clear of the pit of human opinion.
I have such a desire to please others. Please keep my eyes
and heart focused only on You. In Jesus' name I pray, amen.

SHELTERED IN
HIS ARMS

My salvation and my significance depend ultimately on God;
the core of my strength, my shelter, is in the True God.
Have faith in Him in all circumstances, dear people. Open up
your heart to Him; the True God shelters us in His arms.
PSALM 62:7–8 VOICE

There are few images we can conjure up more powerful than that of being sheltered in God's arms. When we're overwhelmed by life and feeling the weight of hopelessness, knowing we have a safe place makes all the difference in the world. Knowing we are loved matters!

It takes faith to believe this kind of love and compassion is possible. To really trust that God is foundational to your life in every way and wants only good is often hard to believe. And then having confidence that He'll bring you through the mess sometimes feels like a pie-in-the-sky dream. Faith is choosing to believe anyway. It's choosing to open your heart to Him regardless. And stepping out of your comfort zone to trust Him rewards you with salvation and significance.

Father, picturing myself in Your lap and wrapped in Your strong arms does
so much for my heart. Sometimes I feel alone and worthless, overwhelmed
by the stress and strife I'm facing. Knowing that my faith unlocks Your
blessing means the world to me. In Jesus' name I pray, amen.

WHOM DO YOU RELY ON?

*An arrogant and greedy man stirs up strife, but he who trusts in
the LORD will be blessed and prosper. He who trusts confidently
in his own heart is a [dull, thickheaded] fool, but he who
walks in [skillful and godly] wisdom will be rescued.*

PROVERBS 28:25–26 AMP

There is so much wisdom in these proverbs. They do a great job of
contrasting the differences between relying on the Lord and depending
on yourself. Every day you have to make this kind of choice a million
times. Every situation you're in, every problem you face, every challenge
that comes your way, you get to decide if your faith will be anchored
in God or in your own humanity.

Scripture tells us that when we choose to trust God instead of
clamoring for control, we will find success—even if success looks different than what we had imagined. We will be protected and rescued.
But if we don't, if we follow through with the power grab, trouble will
no doubt come our way. We will be foolish and reckless. Let's choose
to be women full of faith in the Lord, trusting His plan for our life.

*Father, thank You for making me smart and capable. And in the same vein,
thank You for making me unable to live my life well without Your help.
I don't want to rely on myself knowing my limitations. Instead, I want
to fully place my faith in You! In Jesus' name I pray, amen.*

AN INVITATION TO
KNOW HIM BETTER

*He who deals wisely and heeds [God's] word and counsel
shall find good, and whoever leans on, trusts in, and is
confident in the Lord—happy, blessed, and fortunate is he.*

PROVERBS 16:20 AMPC

God's Word is an invitation to know Him better. It's through the Bible that the Lord reveals Himself to you. It's how He teaches you what righteous living looks like and trains You to live and love well. It's through the Word you are challenged to choose a different path to walk. And it's packed with powerful truths designed to make your life full of passion and purpose. Even more, it's alive and relevant to any and every situation you face today.

When you let the Bible guide your steps, your faith grows deep roots as you learn about the God you serve. Heeding the counsel in its pages enriches your life on every level. And it not only pleases the Lord, but it brings you a lasting happiness able to withstand even the toughest storms that may come your way. Let faith be your driving force as you navigate the challenges of life.

*Father, thank You for the Word. I'm so grateful to have a tangible
reminder of Your faithfulness. Let it be my go-to resource for
righteous living, the place I find truth and instruction every time I
open its pages. Use it to grow my faith! In Jesus' name I pray, amen.*

STARTING WITH FAITH

Make me hear of Your faithful love in the morning, for I trust in You.
Teach me how I should walk, for I offer my soul up to You.
Psalm 143:8 voice

What is the first thing you do in the morning? Maybe you brush your teeth or take a shower. Maybe you lace up your shoes and go for a walk or run or grab your phone and scroll through all the notifications left throughout the night. Or do you beeline it to the kitchen for your favorite breakfast? But what if your morning routine started with the Lord?

We all know that what you do in the morning sets the tone for the day. It matters. And when you get right with God before the busyness starts, you are making the wise choice of setting yourself up for goodness! It's a decision to activate your faith as a shield of protection for what the day may bring. And the Lord will honor that decision in ways you can't even imagine! Rise and shine and choose to start with faith.

Father, I want to set myself up for Your goodness and generosity every day. Remind me as I wake up each morning to get my heart right with You. Let me start my day with prayer and thanksgiving. And let that be what guides the rest of my schedule! In Jesus' name I pray, amen.

WHY WE DON'T HAVE TO PANIC

"Don't panic. I'm with you. There's no need to fear
for I'm your God. I'll give you strength. I'll help you.
I'll hold you steady, keep a firm grip on you."
Isaiah 41:10 MSG

So often, our first response to scary news is panic. When our deepest feelings about someone or something are exposed, we get flustered. Our insecurities rear their ugly heads, causing anxiety and fear. When we begin to forecast our situation, inevitably predicting horrible outcomes and endings, it can be unnerving. Panic is a response to the unpredictability of life.

The truth is, we cannot always keep it at bay. It has a special way of sneaking up and biting us. But you know what we can do? We can be quick to see it and even quicker to take that rattling to the Lord. He is the only One who can calm our nerves and steady our foundation. When we believe in faith that He is the divine antidote to the panic we often feel, we will find peaceful waters in the storm.

Father, thank You for making a way so panic doesn't have to pull us under.
I may not always be able to stop the anxiety when it sneaks up on me,
but I can activate my faith as I cry out to You for help. Please keep me
steady. Please hold on to me. I need You! In Jesus' name I pray, amen.

HE RECOGNIZES YOU

*The LORD is good, a strength and stronghold in
the day of trouble; He knows [He recognizes, cares for,
and understands fully] those who take refuge and trust in Him.*
NAHUM 1:7 AMP

Your willingness to exercise your faith does not go unnoticed. When you choose to stand up and trust the Lord with your situation, He sees it. God is always watching you, not in a creepy way, but in a protective way. His eyes never divert from you, sweet one. Your Father in heaven fixes His gaze on His prize creation. . .and that includes you.

Every time you activate your faith, it pleases the Lord. It delights His heart to know you chose to believe in His plan over your own. God is so trustworthy and faithful, and His hope is that you will cry out to Him for strength in hard times. Why not let the Lord be your refuge in those times you feel attacked? Let Him be your stronghold when you feel weak. Let Him care for you when you're scared. Anytime you stand confident in God, He recognizes the faith it took to do so.

●

*Father, I know You are good and trustworthy. I know Your heart
for me is always good. Give me the courage to exercise my faith in
times of need rather than trust in myself. And thank You for noticing
all the times I reach out to You for help. In Jesus' name I pray, amen.*

THE CHALLENGE TO TRUST TOTALLY

Go ahead and make all the plans you want, but it's the Lord who will ultimately direct your steps. We are all in love with our own opinions, convinced they're correct. But the Lord is in the midst of us, testing and probing our every motive. Before you do anything, put your trust totally in God and not in yourself.

PROVERBS 16:1–3 TPT

God gave you a creative mind, full of ideas and able to make plans for the future. He encourages forward motion and loves to see His children embracing their giftings. God loves when you dream about what may be. He delights in your excitement for what can be. So, grab hold of your hopes and dreams with gusto!

But at the same time, choose to seek His wisdom. In faith, ask the Lord to confirm your next steps. Ask for His favor to be upon you. Let Him explore your heart and your motives, making sure they are aligned with His will. God is giving you the freedom to plan as He challenges you to trust Him through it.

Father, sometimes I think I know it all. I am in love with my opinions and ideas. But more than that, I want to crave to be in Your will. Give me the confidence to make decisions for my future and give me the faith to follow You no matter what. In Jesus' name I pray, amen.

WHOM WILL YOU TRUST?

*"Cursed is the strong one who depends on mere humans, who thinks
he can make it on muscle alone and sets God aside as dead weight.
He's like a tumbleweed on the prairie, out of touch with the good earth.
He lives rootless and aimless in a land where nothing grows."*

JEREMIAH 17:5–6 MSG

Oh friend, please don't miss the strong warning these verses provide.
There are no minced words found here. This passage of scripture isn't
confusing or up for interpretation. There's no way to soften this truth
so it's more palatable. And in faith, we would be full of wisdom and
discernment to walk this out every day.

Jeremiah is setting us up for goodness by steering us away from
a common trap we have all fallen into from time to time. He knows
the failure rate of those who decide to put their trust in mankind above
God. He understands all the ways we'll fall flat on our face when we
choose to depend on people for answers we should look to the Lord
for. He sees the compounded hopelessness we will experience when
we ignore the Lord's help as we try our best to navigate life. God is not
dead weight to ignore. He is solid counsel to embrace!

*Father, grow my faith so You become my default button. I want You
to be my first stop when I am in need. In Jesus' name I pray, amen.*

IT TAKES GRIT AND GRACE

My enemies say, "You are nothing!" Even my friends and neighbors hold me in contempt! They dread seeing me and they look the other way when I pass by. I am totally forgotten, buried away like a dead man, discarded like a broken dish thrown in the trash. I overheard their whispered threats, the slander of my enemies. I'm terrified as they plot and scheme to take my life. I'm desperate, Lord! I throw myself upon you, for you alone are my God!

PSALM 31:11–14 TPT

God loves you. Others may not, but He always has and always will. There will be plenty of times in your life that today's verse will be an appropriate description of how you're feeling. Maybe it already has. Life has a way of beating us up and making us doubt our worth. It can knock us to our knees as we grapple with our goodness. And there are some mean-spirited people who think nothing of spewing hateful words when we step out of their favor. It's takes grit and grace to walk out this life. And it takes a whole lot of faith-filled choices to not let it discourage us.

Father, I'm tired of feeling tossed about because of circumstances and people. I'm tired of dealing with hatefulness. Would You please comfort me and encourage my weary heart? Would You remind me of who I am to You? In Jesus' name I pray, amen.

WHEN FRIENDS
BETRAY AND BREAK

I was betrayed by my friend, though I lived in peace with him. While he was stretching out his hand of friendship, he was secretly breaking every promise he had ever made to me! His words were smooth and charming. Yet his heart was disloyal and full of hatred—his words soft as silk while all the time scheming my demise. So here's what I've learned through it all: Leave all your cares and anxieties at the feet of the Lord, and measureless grace will strengthen you.

PSALM 55:20–22 TPT

Chances are you've had a friendship go south. Maybe it was a friend who you thought would be there through thick and thin. Maybe it was one who had walked out hard situations beside you, helping you confidently navigate them. Or perhaps it was someone who had cared for your heart as much as you cared for theirs. Friends are so important, and it hurts when we lose them.

God knows the value of community because He created us for it. And when we face a betrayal or break with friends, He promises to exchange His comfort for our hurt. When we take our pain to Him, the Lord says He will strengthen us and give us grace. Let Him care for your broken heart.

Father, I'm asking for Your supernatural healing. I need to climb in Your lap for comfort. Please help me. In Jesus' name I pray, amen.

FIGHT LIKE A HERO

Give us a father's help when we face our enemies. For to
trust in any man is an empty hope. With God's help we will
fight like heroes and he will trample down our every foe!
PSALM 60:11–12 TPT

When you fight like a hero, it means you are battling from a place of strength. You are standing up for yourself with confidence, knowing you will be victorious in the end. It means you are full of courage, even if the situation feels scary and the odds seem stacked against you. Fighting like a hero can only be done with faith.

Where do you need to be the protagonist in your story? In what relationship are you struggling to fight with conviction? Where do you need endurance for what's ahead? Every solution to these areas will be filled by the Lord. Too often we rely on our own strength or in the strength of others to fix things, but scripture tells us that is an empty hope. God is the reason we can fight like a hero, confident a win is around the corner.

●

Father, give me courage to fight like a hero for me and those I care
about. Build my confidence in You to be my source. Help me stand
in faith when life gets hard rather than cower in fear. I trust You to
give me everything I need to live in victory. In Jesus' name I pray, amen.

HELP ME WITH
MY DOUBTS!

He asked the boy's father, "How long has this been going on?"
"Ever since he was a little boy. Many times it pitches him into fire or
the river to do away with him. If you can do anything, do it. Have a
heart and help us!" Jesus said, "If? There are no 'ifs' among believers.
Anything can happen." No sooner were the words out of his mouth
than the father cried, "Then I believe. Help me with my doubts!"
MARK 9:21–24 MSG

This father was desperate for help. His son had been possessed with a demon for years, and he was looking for Jesus to cast it out so he could be free. We can assume this man heard stories of healing, which is why he sought Him out. He had faith that Jesus could do something miraculous. He believed the Lord was able to do what others had not, and he knew Jesus was the last hope for his son.

God was so gracious to include this story in the Bible because it speaks right to our doubt. We may know that God is all-powerful and all-knowing from a distance, but it can sometimes be a different story when it becomes personal. We have full faith until we have to have full faith for our situation. Amen? When you begin to doubt He will come through for you, ask God to increase your faith.

Father, help me with my doubts!
In Jesus' name I pray, amen.

THE FAITH TO RUN

The believer replied, "Every promise of God proves true; he protects
everyone who runs to him for help. So don't second-guess him;
he might take you to task and show up your lies."
PROVERBS 30:5-6 MSG

Some struggles we face have us crawling to the Lord for help. We are weighed down with insecurities or fear, and we crumble. And sometimes we walk to the Lord with our troubles. Not quite feeling the urgency yet, but we know we'll eventually need His help so we start heading His direction. But then there are times we run because we know God is our only hope, and we are desperate.

What if instead of crawling or walking, we ran every time we needed the Father's help? What if we let Him be the first voice to speak into our situation? What if we had enough faith to trust Him with everything that threatened our peace? What if we believed His promises were real and true, and for us? What if we chose to be women who run to the Lord for protection, confident He will meet our needs? Let's do it.

●

Father, I want You to be my destination when life gets hard. I want You to
be my first thought when I am afraid or insecure. Give me the confidence
to run to You for help and hope. Grow my faith. In Jesus' name I pray, amen.

UNCHANGING

Jesus the Anointed One is always the same:
yesterday, today, and forever.
HEBREWS 13:8 VOICE

We live in a world of constant change. Learning to be flexible and to go with the flow is a vital life skill because nothing remains unaltered. Maybe you thought your marriage was forever, but divorce happened. Maybe you're eager to give up your single status and find a spouse, but you are still here. Or perhaps your job description has morphed into something you don't like, or the epic farmland behind your home was just bought for development. Maybe the relationship with your kids isn't as sweet as before, or your yearly physical shows a significant change in your health. Maybe your positive outlook on life has disappeared. In this world change is inevitable.

How wonderful then to know that God is unchanging. He is the same yesterday, today, and will be tomorrow, providing stability. It means that His love for you isn't conditional. His plans for your life aren't shakable. His ability to intervene isn't affected by anything or anyone. His sovereignty can't be removed. And God's mood is unaffected by the state of the world. It means you can anchor your faith in the Lord with confidence, knowing He is trustworthy in every aspect of your relationship with Him.

Father, thank You for providing stability in an ever-changing world.
Thank You for being a safe place for my heart. In Jesus' name I pray, amen.

THE CALL TO LOVE

Let love continue among you. Don't forget to extend your hospitality to all—even to strangers—for as you know, some have unknowingly shown kindness to heavenly messengers in this way. Remember those imprisoned for their beliefs as if you were their cellmate; and care for any who suffer harsh treatment, as you are all one body.

HEBREWS 13:1–3 VOICE

It takes faith to have this kind of love, especially when we don't feel it's deserved. Caring about those around us can often feel like more of a chore or duty than a desire. And there are days where the only way we can muster these kinds of feelings at all is with the Lord's help.

But because God first loved us, we are now able to extend it to others. On our own, we are inconsistent and conditional. We're easily swayed by our mood or their shortcomings. But when we activate our faith and ask for His help to care for those around us, we can show hospitality and kindness. Faith helps keep us from sitting in judgment of others, deciding who is worthy of our time and who is not. And it allows us to recognize the value of compassion and forgiveness. Ask God for His help to love.

Father, I need Your help to love others well. Grow my faith in You so love naturally flows from it. And help me see them through Your eyes. In Jesus' name I pray, amen.

BOLD AND FREE

*My purpose in writing is simply this: that you who believe
in God's Son will know beyond the shadow of a doubt that you
have eternal life, the reality and not the illusion. And how bold
and free we then become in his presence, freely asking according
to his will, sure that he's listening. And if we're confident that he's
listening, we know that what we've asked for is as good as ours.*
1 John 5:13–15 msg

If you've accepted Jesus as your personal Savior, believing He's the Son of God who died for your sins, then you have eternal life. You've secured your eternity. And it's because of that belief, you can ask the Lord for what you need freely and boldly. You don't have to worry if He is too busy to listen. You don't have to be concerned you're too much or not enough. And there's no perfect phrasing or time of day to pray. What a relief.

Friend, go ahead and dream big; boldly ask for what your heart desires. No request is too large, too small, or too weird. You can have confident faith that He hears your prayers. God is always listening. And because He knows what's best for you, He responds accordingly. Your job is to ask away and then trust that His answer is the best because the Lord's heart for you is always good.

*Father, thanks for the freedom to pray boldly
and freely! In Jesus' name I pray, amen.*

A BEAUTIFUL ACT
OF WORSHIP

*So here's what I want you to do, God helping you: Take your everyday,
ordinary life—your sleeping, eating, going-to-work, and walking-
around life—and place it before God as an offering. Embracing
what God does for you is the best thing you can do for him.*

ROMANS 12:1 MSG

When you live your life in ways that please the Lord, it's a beautiful
act of worship. Did you know that? Those times you chose to tell the
truth all the while knowing it could expose your heart and motives,
you were glorifying God. When you decided to love the unlovable and
forgive the unforgivable rather than sit in judgment, it pleased Him.
Every time you took the righteous path over the easy path your heart
desired, God recognized your pursuit of godly living. And in those
moments where you rerouted your ugly thoughts to scripture, kept
your mouth from saying mean-spirited words, and acted in kindness,
it glorified the Lord.

It takes faith to live like this. It's a choice we make every day to
believe what His Word teaches us as His followers. And it takes grit to
walk it out in every part of our lives.

●

*Father, I want my life to glorify You. I want my choices and decisions
to be acts of worship, revealing my love and appreciation for who
You are and for all You have done in my life. In Jesus' name I pray, amen.*

UNSHAPED BY THE WORLD

Don't become so well-adjusted to your culture that you fit into it without even thinking. Instead, fix your attention on God. You'll be changed from the inside out. Readily recognize what he wants from you, and quickly respond to it. Unlike the culture around you, always dragging you down to its level of immaturity, God brings the best out of you, develops well-formed maturity in you.

ROMANS 12:2 MSG

Place your faith in God, not in what the world can offer you. It's an easy statement to read but a hard one to walk out. Wouldn't you agree? Choosing not to be shaped by the culture and climate of society sometimes feels impossible. We engage in trends, get caught up in what's hot and new on social media, and adopt ideas and opinions from what we read and watch. And deep down, we want to fit in so we feel relevant. Staying unshaped by the world is a venti-sized order that challenges every fiber of our humanity.

But for us to walk out our faith in God. . .for us to discern what His will is for our life. . .we have to keep our hearts turned toward Him. We must train our minds to stay focused on His promises. And when we do, we'll know what is good and pleasing to the Lord and it will bring out the best in us.

Father, I want only You to have influence over my life. In Jesus' name I pray, amen.

HIS PROMISE IN
THE STORMY SEAS

When you face stormy seas I will be there with you with endurance and calm; you will not be engulfed in raging rivers. If it seems like you're walking through fire with flames licking at your limbs, keep going; you won't be burned.

ISAIAH 43:2 VOICE

Friend, let this verse wash over you today. Let it bring much-needed comfort to your weary spirit. Allow these words to calm your anxious heart as it offers a powerful reminder that God will take care of you through the stormy seas you're facing right now.

Because you've put your faith in the Lord, He makes you promises. He promises to be with you no matter the size of waves crashing around you. You may feel adrift from helping hands here—but know without a doubt God is closer than your next breath. And it's His presence that will give you endurance for the stormy waters and a sense of calm as you navigate through them. God promises that you won't get caught in the undertow of the struggles you're facing. You won't get pulled underwater because of your problems. Instead, He will reward your faith by making sure you have everything you need to come out the other side with joy, hope, and strength.

Father, I am so thankful for Your availability. What a gift to know no matter what I'm facing, You've got me. In Jesus' name I pray, amen.

SHAME AND GUILT

So Lord, don't hold back your love or withhold your tender mercies
from me. Keep me in your truth and let your compassion overflow
to me no matter what I face. Evil surrounds me; problems greater
than I can solve come one after another. Without you, I know I can't
make it. My sins are so many! I'm so ashamed to lift my face to you.
For my guilt grabs me and stings my soul until I am weakened and spent.

PSALM 40:11–12 TPT

When we are buried in shame and guilt, it feels almost impossible to
lift our head to the Lord for help. We feel unlovable and worry we've
pushed God too far and are now out of His grace. Embarrassed by our
choices, we hide away from Him rather than activate our faith and
trust Him with our sinfulness.

Are you battling shame and guilt today? Do you feel overwhelmed
by the things you've done wrong? The truth is that we all mess up.
We've all fallen short of the glory of God. But Jesus' blood covers it all,
which means you are never too messy for His love.

Father, help me trust that I am good enough in Your eyes. Remove the shame
and guilt that weigh me down. Open my heart to understand the depth of Your
love for me and give me the confidence to trust it. In Jesus' name I pray, amen.

ONE MORE TIME

*Yet I totally trust you to rescue me one more time, so that I can see
once again how good you are while I'm still alive! Here's what I've
learned through it all: Don't give up; don't be impatient; be entwined
as one with the Lord. Be brave and courageous, and never lose hope.
Yes, keep on waiting—for he will never disappoint you!*

PSALM 27:13–14 TPT

We serve a God of *one more time*. That means we're unable to exhaust
our chances with Him. It means that we'll always get another chance
when we mess up. And this secures the fact that we won't ever be
abandoned by God. He will always show up for you, friend. Whether
you need courage or confidence, hope or healing, or to be rescued or
restored, the Lord will always be there one more time. What a relief
to know that in a world full of unkept promises and destabilizing
uncertainty, you can have faith in God's promise to be available every
time you need Him.

So don't lose hope or give up. Don't be impatient or annoyed that
His answer hasn't been fully revealed yet. Instead, trust that He will
respond at the right moment with the right plan every time.

*Father, what a comfort to know You will always give me another chance.
What a gift to know my messiness won't make You walk away. That gives
me confidence as I wait for You! In Jesus' name I pray, amen.*

BUT THEN YOU REALIZE

I look up to the mountains and hills, longing for God's help. But then I realize that our true help and protection come only from the Lord, our Creator who made the heavens and the earth. He will guard and guide me, never letting me stumble or fall. God is my keeper; he will never forget nor ignore me.

PSALM 121:1–3 TPT

Whom do you look to for help? Do you depend on your husband or boyfriend to make things right? Maybe your best friend is your person. It could be your parents or another family member who feels the most trustworthy. Or do you look to a certain pastor or your work supervisor? Maybe you put your hope in the government or an activist group, or even your workout routine, vitamin regimen, or the good genes you inherited from your parents. The truth is that we all put our faith in something to save us. What about you?

Your faith should compel you to look to the Lord for help. He is the only One who is your true help and protection because He is all-knowing and all-powerful. There is none above Him. No one more capable. No one as loving. And He promises to keep you close as He guides and guards you.

Father, I know there are so many options to cling to, but I choose to put my faith in You! In Jesus' name I pray, amen.

FAITH FOR
THE IMPOSSIBLE

*He never stopped believing God's promise, for he was made
strong in his faith to father a child. And because he was
mighty in faith and convinced that God had all the power
needed to fulfill his promises, Abraham glorified God!*

ROMANS 4:20–21 TPT

Never mind that Abraham was an old man way past his prime and impotent to boot. Forget the fact that Sarah was decades into infertility and by human standards, too old to carry a baby herself. When God spoke to Abraham and said he would father a son, this man of faith didn't even blink an eye. He never questioned the promise that was impossible in the natural. Instead, Abraham jumped right into the goodness of the Lord's favor hook, line, and sinker. Today's verse tells us he never stopped believing God's promise.

What would it take for you to have this kind of faith? The kind where you are convinced God will come through with what He has promised? The kind where you know He can do the improbable? Ask the Lord to increase your willingness and ability to believe in Him. Ask for a greater measure of trust and hope. Ask God to give you faith for the impossible.

*Father, I want to have faith like Abraham, convinced of Your goodness
and power. Forgive my doubts in the past. Would You help me become
unshakable in my trust of Your Word? In Jesus' name I pray, amen.*

OPPOSING FORCES

The thief comes only in order to steal and kill and destroy.
I came that they may have and enjoy life, and have
it in abundance (to the full, till it overflows).

JOHN 10:10 AMPC

There are two forces in the world—good and evil. And every single day, we're faced with both. Our job is to recognize them and respond accordingly. It takes wisdom to know the difference and faith to know how to proceed.

There is an enemy out there who hates you because you belong to God. Actually, he hates God the most, but since he can't destroy Him, we are the next in line. So this enemy—Satan—goes to great lengths to steal from you, kill your hopes and dreams, and destroy your life. But the Lord came for different reasons. He planned a good life for you. This doesn't mean everything will be easy and that you'll be rich and powerful. Instead, it means you will find joy and abundance regardless of your circumstances because of your faith in God. And when the enemy does attack, the Lord promises to bring beauty from the ashes if you will trust Him.

Father, it's hard to imagine that Satan hates me like he does. And knowing his plans are always for my destruction is disheartening and scary. Thank You for wanting more for me. Thank You for wanting my life to overflow with Your goodness. And thank You for being my Protector. In Jesus' name I pray, amen.

HAVE FAITH

*"Look at all the birds—do you think they worry about
their existence? They don't plant or reap or store up food,
yet your heavenly Father provides them each with food.
Aren't you much more valuable to your Father than they?"*

MATTHEW 6:26 TPT

Sometimes we just have to clench our jaw and choose to believe. We have to muster the grit to trust the Lord with our situation even when it feels unnatural. To live with a sense of peace, we must find the courage to grow our faith muscle by flexing it every day. It's not easy, but it's necessary. Friend, having confidence that God will come through isn't for the faint of heart. It's not the easy option because we like to feel in control. It's not often our default button because trying to fix things ourselves feels normal. Faith takes bravery and tenacity.

Today's verse offers some much-needed perspective. It's meant to build our assurance in God's love and provision. It's meant to grow our faith in His care and concern for us. It's designed to build trust, knowing the Lord takes care of those He adores. Never forget, you are valuable!

*Father, I love how much You care for creation. It's encouraging to
know You're active in our everyday lives, making sure we have
what we need. Thank You for taking care of me. What a relief to
realize You always have eyes on me. In Jesus' name I pray, amen.*

THE DEEP ROOTS OF CERTAINTY

Certainly Your faithful protection and loving provision will pursue me where I go, always, everywhere. I will always be with the Eternal, in Your house forever.

PSALM 23:6 VOICE

Do you hear the resolve in the author's words? He is certain of God's protection and provision. He is convinced the Lord will always pursue his heart no matter where life takes him. He is confident there is no place he can hide from God's care. And the writer is positive that he will spend eternity in heaven, surrounded by the glory of the Lord. In all these things, he is certain.

You can have that same certainty because all these assurances are available to you too. This promise is also your promise. And grabbing hold of these is an act of faith that requires a choice. It's a decision to believe that God is alive and active in the details of your life, not only today and tomorrow, but forever. Living with this truth planted deeply in your heart enables you to enjoy freedom from fear and insecurity. And it grows deep, beautiful roots of certainty that will help you weather any storm.

Father, help me grow my faith deep in the soil of Your love. Give me confidence and courage to trust You no matter what comes my way—like second nature. And help me have a deep sense of Your consistency in my life. In Jesus' name I pray, amen.

MORE THAN ENOUGH

The Lord is my best friend and my shepherd. I always have more than enough. He offers a resting place for me in his luxurious love. His tracks take me to an oasis of peace, the quiet brook of bliss. That's where he restores and revives my life. He opens before me pathways to God's pleasure and leads me along in his footsteps of righteousness so that I can bring honor to his name.

PSALM 23:1–3 TPT

It takes faith to follow others. Too often, we rest in our own abilities and scoff at any hint of leadership from anyone else. We can't trust their heart or their motive, worrying they don't have our best in mind. We're concerned they'll take us places uncomfortable or unfamiliar. And because we struggle with trust, we often choose to lead our own way through life, hoping for the best.

The psalmist had a different approach. He chose to trust God. Seeing Him as a friend and shepherd gave him faith to follow His leading, and they experienced rest, peace, bliss, restoration, revival, and a sweet relationship with God along the way. He had more than enough to convince him of His trustworthiness. Why not let the Lord be your guide?

Father, please be my Shepherd and Leader. Sustain and restore me each day, showing me how to live in a right relationship with You. Guide me as I navigate the challenges and joys coming my way. In Jesus' name I pray, amen.

GENERATIONAL FAITH

*Our mothers and fathers trusted in You; they trusted,
and You rescued them. They cried out to You for help and
were spared; they trusted in You and were vindicated.*
PSALM 22:4–5 VOICE

What a beautiful heritage passed down to their children. Faith was solidly established, easy for the younger generation to see, and they remembered. This is the kind of touchstone they would have to rely on for the rest of their lives. Their own experiences would then be added to the ones of their forefathers, making an even stronger case for faith for the next group. Talk about a powerful line of generational blessing.

How about you? Take some time today to peek back in your family line. Find those members who loved the Lord and lived with righteous intention. List the names of those who walked out their faith, visible for all to see. Think about the ones who trusted God to provide, deliver, and heal. And then thank the Lord for them because it was their faith that made an impact on yours. Now it's your turn to pass the torch to the next generation. Let that be a catalyst for intentionality as you walk with God every day.

*Father, thank You for those who came before me and left a beautiful
imprint of faith on my heart. Let me be that for those around me.
Use me to be a generational blessing. In Jesus' name I pray, amen.*

HIS PROMISE THEN IS HIS PROMISE NOW

"This exile is just like the days of Noah for me: I promised then that the waters of Noah would never again flood the earth. I'm promising now no more anger, no more dressing you down. For even if the mountains walk away and the hills fall to pieces, my love won't walk away from you, my covenant commitment of peace won't fall apart." The God who has compassion on you says so.
ISAIAH 54:9–10 MSG

God is incapable of changing. He always has been and always will be. So when you read in the Old Testament that He is all-knowing, He still is. When the New Testament says He is a Strong Tower and Provider, that remains true today. God brings much-needed stability to our chaotic world and peace to our anxious heart. He remains the only One we can always depend on. His love is constant, His provision endless, and His care continuous. He possesses unceasing patience, and His pursuit of our hearts is relentless.

You can safely place your faith in the Lord because He has a long track record of trustworthiness, not only in your life but in humanity. His promises never waver. They never change. He's never inconsistent, and His loyal love for you will never fail.

Father, it does my heart so good to know Your promises are unchanging. Thank You for being steadfast. In Jesus' name I pray, amen.

THE TRUTH ABOUT ANGER

*Go ahead and be angry. You do well to be angry—but don't use your
anger as fuel for revenge. And don't stay angry. Don't go to bed
angry. Don't give the Devil that kind of foothold in your life.*

Ephesians 4:26–27 msg

What a relief to know that anger in and of itself isn't a sin. God blessed us with an array of emotions, and anger is one of them. And honestly, there are things in the world today—things that happen to us— where anger is the appropriate response. But God also knows that if we leave anger unchecked, the enemy will use it to take us out. If we decide to hold on to it, justifying it every chance we get, it will become a stronghold.

What does anger look like in your life? Is it something that fuels you, or an emotion that has its right place and time? Sometimes we don't know, and that's where faith comes in. Ask the Lord to help you navigate the line between appropriate and inappropriate anger. Be willing to trust that He will guide you and keep you in check. And always be aware of the enemy's desire to mess with you. Don't let anger be the way he gains a foothold.

*Father, I need Your help to make sure anger doesn't turn
into something the enemy can use against me. I trust
You to show me. In Jesus' name I pray, amen.*

ROLL YOUR WORKS

*Roll your works upon the Lord [commit and trust them wholly
to Him; He will cause your thoughts to become agreeable to
His will, and] so shall your plans be established and succeed.*

PROVERBS 16:3 AMPC

Go ahead. Plan away! Dream up your next steps. Think through the path you want to traverse. Make preparations for your future. Organize your thoughts. Strategize ideas with others. Blueprint out the flowchart of concepts. Step out of your comfort zone with vision. Go for it! But don't forget to include the Lord, asking for His intervention through the process. Ask for His guidance. Ask Him to give you wisdom to follow His leading and discernment to hear His voice. Include your faith every step of the way, and trust the Lord's prompting.

When your dreams include a desire to hear God's leading, the Word says He will supernaturally cause your thoughts to match up with His will. You won't go rogue, satisfying the fleshy hopes of your humanity. Instead, you will let the Lord transform your plans to align with His will, and He will then establish them and bring success. This is faith in action!

●

*Father, there are so many ideas for my future that I'm chewing on
but will now bring them to You for direction. Give me the ears to hear
Your voice. Thank You for being interested, and for helping me solidify
and secure them with Your favor! In Jesus' name I pray, amen.*

UNAFRAID

Keep your lives free from the love of money, and be content with what you have because He has said, "I will never leave you; I will always be by your side." Because of this promise, we may boldly say, The Lord is my help—I won't be afraid of anything. How can anyone harm me?
HEBREWS 13:5–6 VOICE

God's plan was never for you to live in fear. Because fear isn't from the Lord, His hope is that you will counter it with faith. He wants you to feel so secure with His presence in your life that fear melts away. God made a promise to always be with you. He promises to never leave your side, always present whether it be in your joys or challenges.

What makes you afraid? Right now, what are your fears? What keeps you up at night riddled with worry and anxiety? Is it finances? Relationships? An unknown future? A health scare? Your safety and security? Activate your faith by remembering that God promises to be with you always. Let that truth give you confidence and courage to stay strong regardless of what comes your way.

Father, what a relief for my heart to know You promise to always be with me no matter what. Would You remind me of Your presence in those moments fear takes over? I want to be able to stand in faith, not fear. In Jesus' name I pray, amen.

DON'T MAKE HIM TUG

I hear the Lord saying, "I will stay close to you, instructing and guiding you along the pathway for your life. I will advise you along the way and lead you forth with my eyes as your guide. So don't make it difficult; don't be stubborn when I take you where you've not been before. Don't make me tug you and pull you along. Just come with me!"

PSALM 32:8-9 TPT

What a great visual, yes? Think back to a time when you had to be pushed or pulled to go somewhere. A time when you were reluctant to follow. A situation when you were stubborn, refusing to listen to sound advice. Remember those times when for whatever reason, you didn't want to trust someone who you knew deep down had your best interest in mind. This is exactly what God is asking you not to do with Him.

If there is anyone you can put your full faith in, it's the Lord. He's proven time and time again that He is trustworthy. And in today's verse, He reminds you that He's right with you throughout your day. God wants you to look for His instruction and guidance as He leads you. He wants you to listen to His advice because He's steering you in the right way.

Father, I confess I can be stubborn, but I'm going to change that starting today. I will follow Your lead in my life. In Jesus' name I pray, amen.

BEARING YOUR HEART

Open up before God, keep nothing back; he'll do whatever needs to be done: He'll validate your life in the clear light of day and stamp you with approval at high noon.

Psalm 37:5–6 MSG

Have you ever just laid it out there for God, telling Him every single detail of your worry? Have you opened up with Him in raw and real ways, revealing the deepest parts of your pain? Have you purged your anxious heart of all the reasons you're stuck in fear or insecurity? There is something so powerful about bearing it all to the only One who can fully understand and love you without judgment.

You're invited to open up before the Lord, holding nothing back. Every day, you can be fully transparent before God. It's your faith in Him that makes this possible! It's your faith that encourages His intervention. It's your faith that draws His validation that you are worthy and valuable. And when you choose to trust the Lord with your deepest thoughts and fears, He will give you exactly what's needed to bring hope, help, and healing. It's a scary proposition because we remember times others have judged us, but God's heart for you is always good.

●

Father, it's hard for me to be so vulnerable. I confess that I am afraid of judgment. Would You grow my faith so I can be confident in our relationship, trusting that my messiness won't scare You away? In Jesus' name I pray, amen.

ALL YOUR TRUST

*He who takes refuge in the shelter of the Most High will be
safe in the shadow of the Almighty. He will say to the Eternal,
"My shelter, my mighty fortress, my God, I place all my trust in You."*
PSALM 91:1–2 VOICE

Where do you go for refuge when you feel vulnerable or exposed? Some of us may use food to numb us into a false sense of peace. We may reach for the remote control and lose ourselves as we binge Netflix. We may drink at the end of each day, hoping to calm our anxiety. Maybe we shop online looking for a high from the next buy. We may spend way too much time on social media or play hours of Candy Crush. Some may even avoid any kind of community and hide at home rather than spend quality time with friends or family. Yep, we all have our go-tos.

What if instead, we decided to take the Lord up on His offer to shelter us and provide safety? It takes a leap of faith to trust a fresh wound and an unknown outcome to someone we can't see or touch. And it requires grit to choose faith over fear. Decide to believe God's heart for us is always good, and have confidence He is a safe place to anchor all our trust.

●

Father, I place all my trust in You! In Jesus' name I pray, amen.

DON'T BE A FOOL

Self-confident know-it-alls will prove to be fools. But when you lean on the wisdom from above, you will have a way to escape the troubles of your own making.

PROVERBS 28:26 TPT

There's no doubt we are intelligent women, able to make smart decisions for ourselves and our family. We organize and multitask with the best of them, and we've never met a to-do list we couldn't conquer. We own businesses and run corporations. We've held public offices and managed community activities. We're homeschoolers and daycare providers. The Lord gave us amazing skill sets able to navigate life with confidence. But without God's wisdom, we are limping through life

Be careful not to fall into the know-it-all camp where we run solo. While we may be able to maintain that plan for a time, we will eventually get to the end of ourselves. We'll interject our humanity into the situation too much. We'll make decisions that haven't been well thought out or vetted. And it will backfire in one way or another. Always, always, always include God in your plans. Activate your faith by asking for His wisdom. Big or small, invite the Lord to speak into your decisions. It's the antidote to being foolish.

Father, I confess I rely on my gifts and talents too often. Sometimes I get impatient and move ahead of You. Help me invite You into every decision I face and wait for Your response. In Jesus' name I pray, amen.

TRUST GOD TO BE THE JUDGE

Don't hit back; discover beauty in everyone. If you've got it in you, get along with everybody. Don't insist on getting even; that's not for you to do. "I'll do the judging," says God. "I'll take care of it."
Romans 12:17–19 MSG

Be careful when you're wanting to exact revenge on someone who has hurt you because the Word is clear that it's not your place. God says He will be the one to judge. And as a loving Father, He wants to take care of it on your behalf. What does He ask of you? Don't hit back, discover beauty in others, and get along with everyone. Umm. . .excuse me?

Let's be honest, friend. This is a tall order when our feelings get hurt. When we have been offended, trying to get along is the last thing on our mind. We may not want to physically hit someone who angers us, but we may want to hit with our words. God isn't asking us to be a doormat for others to walk all over. But He is asking that we trust Him to take care of it for us. God wants our heart to stay fleshy, not harden with anger, bitterness, or unforgiveness.

Father, this isn't easy for me to do because my default button is to fight back. Help me step back and let You be the judge instead of me. In Jesus' name I pray, amen.

STAY WITH GOD

I'm sure now I'll see God's goodness in the exuberant earth.
Stay with God! Take heart. Don't quit. I'll say it again: Stay with God.
PSALM 27:13-14 MSG

It's so easy to run from the Lord when things hit the fan. We can either run to Him, falling into His arms a red-hot mess, or we can run away, looking for earthly options to make us feel better. The truth is that sometimes we forget He loves us. We forget He's fully aware of our needs. We question God, wondering why harm comes our way. We decide He's against us rather than for us and doubt His goodness.

But friend, those thoughts couldn't be further from the truth of who God is and what He thinks of you. It takes faith to choose truth over lies. But when you spend time in the Word and recount the blessings you've seen in your life and the lives of others, it's hard to justify turning your back on Him. God's track record is perfect. He's always met you right where you were and guided you through the muck. He's blessed you and provided for your needs. He's been good to you, even when He answered differently than you expected. That's why you stay with God no matter what.

Father, forgive me for the times I've run from You. From today forward,
You will be my first stop for everything! In Jesus' name I pray, amen.

VICTORY ON THE OTHER SIDE

Blessed [happy, spiritually prosperous, favored by God] is the man who is steadfast under trial and perseveres when tempted; for when he has passed the test and been approved, he will receive the [victor's] crown of life which the Lord has promised to those who love Him.

JAMES 1:12 AMP

What do you do when trials and temptations come rolling in? Some give up, feeling unmatched for the battle. Some play the victim as they try to milk sympathy for all it's worth. Others may stand in weak pride, all talk and no bite, cowering when the pressure becomes too much. And then there are those who draw their strength from the Lord, knowing He is key to their success. So which camp do you find yourself in most often?

Here's what God wants you to know: when you're steadfast and persevere in those hard moments, holding on to your belief that you can make it through with the Lord's help, you'll find a blessing waiting. Knowing God is for you and working all things for your good creates happiness. Faith makes you favored by Him. And your unwavering trust comes with a promise of victory on the other side.

Father, I appreciate that You offer incentives to those who choose to trust You in the hard moments. I love knowing my obedience is not only recognized, but also rewarded. Help me see the bigger picture of faith. In Jesus' name I pray, amen.

WHITE KNUCKLE YOUR FREEDOM

*Let me be clear, the Anointed One has set us free—not partially,
but completely and wonderfully free! We must always cherish this
truth and stubbornly refuse to go back into the bondage of our past.*

GALATIANS 5:1 TPT

What keeps you from grabbing onto your freedom and holding it with all you've got? Why do you so easily fall back into the patterns of slavery that suck the life out of you? Why do you continually fall back into old patterns that leave you feeling like a failure? Deep breath, friend. These questions are for every single one of us because we all share the tendency to put the chains back on our own wrists. But it doesn't have to be this way.

God is challenging you to white knuckle the freedom you've received. Sometimes we have to hold it with all we've got. We have to believe it's ours for the taking, activating our faith to access His strength so we can walk it out. What a beautiful gift you've been given. Don't let anyone—not even yourself—take it away.

●

*Father, thank You for the gift of freedom through Your Son. Too often
I forget, or I feel unworthy of it, so I choose to stay trapped in my fear
and insecurities. It keeps me from living my best life and I lose out on
experiencing Your goodness. Give me courage to fully accept the
freedom You have for me! In Jesus' name I pray, amen.*

A FAITH BUILDER

Let the words from the book of the law be always on your lips. Meditate on them day and night so that you may be careful to live by all that is written in it. If you do, as you make your way through this world, you will prosper and always find success. This is My command: be strong and courageous. Never be afraid or discouraged because I am your God, the Eternal One, and I will remain with you wherever you go.

JOSHUA 1:8–9 VOICE

God's Word is a faith builder. Its pages are filled with encouragement and truth that bolsters you when you need it the most. It offers scriptures that fill your heart with confidence and courage, sending you back into battle with the assurance of His presence. There are stories of everyday people, relatable to circumstances you face even now. God reveals Himself in the Bible's pages and unpacks His heart for His children. It's a book that is both mysterious and practical for everyday living. And this is why He wants you to spend time reading it.

The Lord's desire is to walk through life with you. Reading His Word helps you recognize His will and plan created just for you. The more you know God, the stronger and more courageous you'll feel because His promises will be on your heart.

●

Father, thank You for encouraging me to know Your Word in my heart. It's power-packed with faith-building encouragement. . .just what I need. In Jesus' name I pray, amen.

SHARING FAITH WITH THE YOUNGER

*That precious memory triggers another: your honest faith—and what
a rich faith it is, handed down from your grandmother Lois to your
mother Eunice, and now to you! And the special gift of ministry you
received when I laid hands on you and prayed—keep that ablaze! God
doesn't want us to be shy with his gifts, but bold and loving and sensible.*

2 TIMOTHY 1:5–7 MSG

One of the most powerful results of being a woman of faith is that
we model it for others. Through our words and actions, we are priv-
ileged to reflect Jesus to those we love and care for. Some may think
of that as a burden, but it's not. We're not expected to be perfect. And
sometimes our vulnerability with the struggles we face matters most
because others get to see our steadfastness. We provide an example
of radical faith instead over fear. Our patience teaches others to wait
on God, trusting His timing and plan. What an honor to pass faith on!

Think about those you influence. What are you teaching them? What
kind of faith are you encouraging them to have? Keep in mind that your
life is demonstrating the level of trust you have in the Lord. Live well!

*Father, help the ways I live and love impact others so they
see You! I want my life to reflect Your goodness and make
a powerful case for faith. In Jesus' name I pray, amen.*

TRUSTING GOD TO MAKE UP THE DIFFERENCE

*Keep your eyes open, hold tight to your convictions,
give it all you've got, be resolute, and love without stopping.*
1 CORINTHIANS 16:13–14 MSG

This is epic advice for living with intention. It's not easy—not by a mile. Choosing to walk this out in your day takes a little grit and a whole lotta faith, because these are not things that come easily. We have to be mindful every step of the way. But when we ask the Lord for the confidence and courage for faith-filled living, we will receive it.

Keeping your eyes open is a brave move. It means you don't cower in fear, but trust God instead. Holding to your convictions means you don't compromise what you know is right and true. Giving it your all demands perseverance and endurance, and loving without stopping is the definition of unconditional. And friend, every bit of this requires faith. Our humanity has limitations, but we can trust God to make up the difference. In your marriage, as you parent, within your community, as you work, with your finances, in how you choose to live life, ask the Lord for His unwavering help.

*Father, thank You for this challenge to live and love well. I realize it's
something that requires Your guidance and support. Give me the tools I
need to live with this kind of intentionality. And would You give me the
faith to know You'll make up the difference? In Jesus' name I pray, amen.*

NEVER ABANDONED

Jesus answered them, "Do you finally believe? In fact, you're about to make a run for it—saving your own skins and abandoning me. But I'm not abandoned. The Father is with me. I've told you all this so that trusting me, you will be unshakable and assured, deeply at peace. In this godless world you will continue to experience difficulties. But take heart! I've conquered the world."
JOHN 16:31–33 MSG

God is always with you. In the good times where everything is falling into place, He is there. In the times where it feels like a train has run you over, God is there. When you are scared and worried about your current situation, you're not alone. When your insecurities are off the chart and have left you feeling unworthy, He is right next to you. Anytime you need strength or courage, the Lord is there to meet those needs. In those moments where you want to give up, God will hold you up. There is never a place you are that He isn't.

So remember when you feel abandoned by those you expected to be beside you, the Lord is there. He will never leave you to be alone when you need help. You won't ever be without His support and care. God is with you every step of the way.

●

Father, what a comfort to know You are always with me no matter what. In Jesus' name I pray, amen.

SUIT UP!

*Put on God's complete set of armor provided for us, so that you will
be protected as you fight against the evil strategies of the accuser!
Your hand-to-hand combat is not with human beings, but with the highest
principalities and authorities operating in rebellion under the heavenly
realms. For they are a powerful class of demon-gods and evil spirits that
hold this dark world in bondage. Because of this, you must wear all the
armor that God provides so you're protected as you confront the slanderer,
for you are destined for all things and will rise victorious.*

EPHESIANS 6:11–13 TPT

When you put on the complete set of God's armor, you are activating
your faith. It's a deliberate decision to protect yourself from the strategies and ploys of the enemy. It's recognizing that your battle isn't
against flesh and blood but instead against those principalities who
oppose God. And suiting up offers you safety and security against the
evil forces bent on destroying your life.

Before your feet hit the floor in the morning, ask the Lord to cover
you with His protection by way of His armor. Believe that by doing this,
you are fully equipped to handle whatever the enemy may throw your
direction. Your protection matters to God!

*Father, I am praying for the full armor right now. Please cover me
with Your provision so I can stand strong against the forces of evil.
I need Your fortification every day. In Jesus' name I pray, amen.*

SECURE IN YOUR FAITH

They will not live in fear or dread of what may come, for their hearts are firm, ever secure in their faith. Steady and strong, they will not be afraid, but will calmly face their every foe until they all go down in defeat.

PSALM 112:7-8 TPT

What does it mean to be secure in your faith? It means that you don't have to be afraid of the future. You don't have to dread what comes next. Why? Because you are protected by your Father who is always looking out for you. Does it mean hard things won't happen? Does it mean there is nothing scary ahead? No. Scripture guarantees that life will be full of trials and tribulations. But you can be secure knowing that God is with you and for you.

When you are secure in Him, it allows you to stand strong. You're confident. You may get knocked down, but you aren't down for long because you know God has you. This mindset allows you to live from a place of strength. It keeps your eyes trained on the Lord rather than your circumstances. And it settles your anxious heart, assured that you are loved and cared for.

Father, give me the courage to secure my faith firmly in You. Strengthen my resolve to trust in You when situations threaten to shake me. And when I am scared or worried, remind me I am protected. In Jesus' name I pray, amen.

THE GREAT HELPER

The Father is sending a great Helper, the Holy Spirit, in My name to teach you everything and to remind you of all I have said to you. My peace is the legacy I leave to you. I don't give gifts like those of this world. Do not let your heart be troubled or fearful.

JOHN 14:26–27 VOICE

Jesus promised a great Helper would come into the world when He departed—the Holy Spirit. And His job is to support those who love the Lord as they grow in their faith and share the Gospel with others. He came to teach and speak the things of God into the hearts of believers to build their faith. And He came to remind believers of what they had already heard, bringing up key encouragement from their time with Jesus.

The Holy Spirit is still alive and active today. If you're a believer in Jesus, God's Spirit is in you right now. He is that gut feeling that points you toward godly living when you have a choice to make. He is the One who encourages you into community with the Lord when you'd rather hide away. He's the One who reminds you to trust God for the peace you're desperate for. And it's the Holy Spirit that helps you grow in your faith.

Father, thank You for sending the Holy Spirit to help me navigate life and increase my faith! In Jesus' name I pray, amen.

HE'S THERE IN
THE SINKING

Peter shouted out, "Lord, if it's really you, then have me join you on the water!" "Come and join me," Jesus replied. So Peter stepped out onto the water and began to walk toward Jesus. But when he realized how high the waves were, he became frightened and started to sink. "Save me, Lord!" he cried out.

MATTHEW 14:28–30 TPT

There is a huge lesson in this verse for all believers. It's a powerful display of what faith can do for us. But it also carries a warning of what happens when we focus too much on our circumstances instead. Take a minute to reread today's scripture and make note of what stands out to you the most.

It's easy to be full of faith when the waters of life are calm. We can trust the Lord when any storms are far off in the distance. But it takes a lot of grit and big confidence to step outside of our safe place to do something that feels impossible. And in those times we venture out and sink in our doubts, the Lord is right there to pull us up every time.

●

Father, help my faith in You be consistent, so the times of sinking are fewer and further between. Help me keep my eyes on You and not the circumstances that threaten to pull me under. And thank You for being there to rescue me when they do. In Jesus' name I pray, amen.

HE WILL ALWAYS
BE THERE

So who can separate us? What can come between us and the love
of God's Anointed? Can troubles, hardships, persecution, hunger,
poverty, danger, or even death? The answer is, absolutely nothing.
As the psalm says, On Your behalf, our lives are endangered constantly;
we are like sheep awaiting slaughter. But no matter what comes,
we will always taste victory through Him who loved us.

ROMANS 8:35–37 VOICE

Think back to a broken relationship that hit where it hurt the most. Maybe it was a marriage that ended in divorce when you prayed it would heal. Maybe a child walked away in defiance and nothing seemed to bring them back around. Maybe a friendship you thought would last forever ended with betrayal and you're grieving its loss. Did someone walk away because they thought you were too messy? In their opinion, were you too frustrating? Did someone say you weren't smart enough or were unable to keep up with the Joneses? Big hugs, friend.

Here's good news for a broken heart: there's nothing you can do to make God break up with you. You're incapable of making Him walk away. Whether you're a hot mess or all put together, you're adored. And when you think you don't fit in, remember you're perfect in His eyes. Ask Him for the faith to believe it.

Father, what a relief to know there's nothing I can be or do
that will separate me from You. In Jesus' name I pray, amen.

THE NEED FOR ENCOURAGEMENT

So stand up! Helping us follow the law is now your responsibility. Do not be afraid; we will support your actions. So Ezra stood up and persuaded the leading priests, the Levites, and all Israel to swear an oath to banish their foreign wives and foreign children. When everyone had taken the oath, he entered the temple chamber of Jehohanan (son of Eliashib) and continued mourning the exiles' unfaithfulness by fasting from food and water.

EZRA 10:4–6 VOICE

Sometimes we need a push to stand strong in our faith and do what we feel God is asking. It may come easy for some, but if you are a little weak-kneed at times and lack courage, you are not alone. Walking out your faith is a daily choice that requires guts and grit at times. Maybe that's why the Lord built us for community. Maybe He knew how much we would need that encouragement. Sometimes what we need the most to live a faith-filled life is a few friends and family to remind us that we are able. We need to know we have what it takes to do what God is asking.

Father, I am one of those who regularly needs to be encouraged to stand in my faith by those around me. It does something for my heart to know I am supported, and it grows my confidence and courage to be obedient to Your leading. In Jesus' name I pray, amen.

BRAVE AND COURAGEOUS
FOR THE SAKE

*"Be brave! We must be courageous for the sake of our people
and the cities of our God. The LORD will do what is good in his eyes."*
2 SAMUEL 10:12 CEB

Have you ever thought about how important it is for others to see us be brave when faced with scary things? It not only bolsters their confidence to deal with what's in front of them, but it also helps to increase their faith that God will come through. Your courage makes a difference in your life and in the lives of those around you.

So when the diagnosis comes and it's not what you'd hoped for, be brave as you navigate the appointments and treatments. When your marriage is a mess and your kids are stressed about it, speak with confidence your trust in God. When your finances are overwhelming and you're struggling to make ends meet, believe in the Lord as your Provider. When life continues to hit you in the gut over and over again, find the courage to follow His path through the valley. Because when you do, your life preaches faith to those around you.

*Father, thank You for the reminder that my level of faith has the
power to impact others. I want to show my family and friends that
You're trustworthy and faithful in all things. Help me put my hope in
You so I encourage them to do the same. In Jesus' name I pray, amen.*

THIS IS WHY

The Lord your God is in the midst of you, a Mighty One, a Savior [Who saves]!
He will rejoice over you with joy; He will rest [in silent satisfaction]
and in His love He will be silent and make no mention [of past sins,
or even recall them]; He will exult over you with singing.
ZEPHANIAH 3:17 AMPC

This is why you can trust the Lord with your life and be yourself rather than strive to become more presentable or acceptable. This is why you don't have to sit in shame for past mistakes. This is why you don't have to crumble under pressure. And friend, this is why you never have to feel alone.

If you don't have it, ask God to bless you with the faith needed to stand firm in today's verse. It's power-packed with truth designed to increase your confidence in Him and in who He made you to be. Be encouraged knowing God is ever present in your life, that your sins are forgotten, and that you delight Him into singing. Let these blessings grow your faith in new and fresh ways. And thank the Lord for loving you so deeply.

Father, I am so grateful for You. Sometimes it's hard to accept that I
could mean this much to someone, but I am choosing to believe Your
words as true and Your love for me as real. In Jesus' name I pray, amen.

TRANSFERRED AND GUARANTEED

Our faith in Jesus transfers God's righteousness to us and he now declares us flawless in his eyes. This means we can now enjoy true and lasting peace with God, all because of what our Lord Jesus, the Anointed One, has done for us. Our faith guarantees us permanent access into this marvelous kindness that has given us a perfect relationship with God. What incredible joy bursts forth within us as we keep on celebrating our hope of experiencing God's glory!

ROMANS 5:1–2 TPT

How cool is it that when you choose to believe Jesus is the Son of God and died for your sins, that act of belief transfers the righteousness of God onto you? In other words, your faith has made you flawless to the Father. Even more, it's also guaranteed you unending access in your relationship with Him. There is no barrier between the two of you—nothing to keep you from experiencing His goodness in your life every day.

In a world filled with heartache and pain, let this be a source of joy. Grab hold of these promises and let them fuel your hope. Embrace your faith so you can find peace and comfort no matter what may come your way.

Father, I love that my choice to believe in Jesus opens up a beautiful life of faith for me. Help me live in that victory every moment of every day, trusting You to meet my needs. In Jesus' name I pray, amen.

THE DOMINO EFFECT

But that's not all! Even in times of trouble we have a joyful confidence, knowing that our pressures will develop in us patient endurance. And patient endurance will refine our character, and proven character leads us back to hope. And this hope is not a disappointing fantasy, because we can now experience the endless love of God cascading into our hearts through the Holy Spirit who lives in us!

ROMANS 5:3–5 TPT

Here's where your faith will grow you into a warrior if you'll let it. But a little disclaimer: this isn't an easy road to walk. It isn't easy, but it's well worth it.

Notice the domino effect in today's verse as one choice builds on the next. When you decide to go all in with the Lord, something beautiful happens. He promises to use everything in your life for His glory and your benefit. He wastes no opportunity to grow you into the faith-filled woman He created you to be. And if you'll allow it, pressures result in endurance that will refine your character and lead you back to hope.

Even more, keep in mind that hope is a powerful component of faith—faith that proves over and over again that God will never disappoint us.

Father, what a privilege to have You constantly refining me and my faith. Only You could create such a powerful domino effect with the hardships I'm going to face in life. Thank You! In Jesus' name I pray, amen.

REAPING WHAT YOU SOW

Make no mistake about it, God will never be mocked! For what you plant will always be the very thing you harvest. The harvest you reap reveals the seed that was planted. If you plant the corrupt seeds of self-life into this natural realm, you can expect to experience a harvest of corruption. If you plant the good seeds of Spirit-life you will reap the beautiful fruits that grow from the everlasting life of the Spirit. And don't allow yourselves to be weary or disheartened in planting good seeds, for the season of reaping the wonderful harvest you've planted is coming!

GALATIANS 6:7–9 TPT

There is an extraordinary relationship between how we choose to live and love. . .and the future results of those decisions. The world may call it karma, but God refers to it as the concept of reaping what we sow.

It works like this: if you choose to sow seeds of kindness into your relationships, the crop you will eat later will reflect that. Sow seeds of faith and watch yours grow. Sow generosity now and harvest it later. The same truths hold if you scatter seeds of hate, bitterness, unforgiveness, and selfishness. Let this principle of sowing and reaping encourage you to be intentional with how you live and love. Let faith inspire your life to glorify Him.

Father, what a powerful concept. I can appreciate that there's a blessing on the other side of intentional living. Thank You for that! In Jesus' name I pray, amen.

THE GIFT OF COMMUNITY

So let's not allow ourselves to get fatigued doing good. At the right
time we will harvest a good crop if we don't give up, or quit. Right now,
therefore, every time we get the chance, let us work for the benefit of all,
starting with the people closest to us in the community of faith.
GALATIANS 6:9–10 MSG

The Lord wants us to love on and be kind to others, but especially our brothers and sisters in the faith. He wants us to stand together through the hard times and celebrate in the good. The truth is that God made us for community. It's a gift. And while we may get frustrated with others, the Lord didn't create us to live alone. We might be more of an introvert, but that's not an excuse to hide out. He wants us to work together, encouraging and affirming as needed.

You may be the exact medicine someone needs to make it another day. You might be the reason they get up, wipe off the dust, and try again. Your words could make all the difference to someone's heartache. Your presence matters. Love them well.

Father, sometimes community is tricky for me. I get hurt or offended and
the last thing I want is to hang out with people. Would You give me
perspective, forgiveness, and grace so I don't allow anything to
keep me from loving others? In Jesus' name I pray, amen.

BE LIKE CALEB

"We went to the land to which you sent us and, oh! It does flow with milk and honey! Just look at this fruit! The only thing is that the people who live there are fierce, their cities are huge and well fortified. Worse yet, we saw descendants of the giant Anak. Amalekites are spread out in the Negev; Hittites, Jebusites, and Amorites hold the hill country; and the Canaanites are established on the Mediterranean Sea and along the Jordan." Caleb interrupted, called for silence before Moses and said, "Let's go up and take the land—now. We can do it."
NUMBERS 13:27–30 MSG

Even though God had promised the Israelites this land was to be theirs, the moment they laid eyes on the people and the cities. . .they freaked out. Doubt crept in as they noticed the size and ferocity of both. And to them, it was a deal breaker. A lack of faith threatened to keep them from taking the land. But Caleb weighed in on the situation. He knew if God was for them and they were following His plan, the Lord's promises would come to be. His faith never wavered.

Let's be women who stand strong in our belief. Let's know His promises by spending time in the Word. And let's take the next step of faith even if it's scary.

Father, I want faith like Caleb. Help me trust in Your promises regardless of what my situation may look like. In Jesus' name I pray, amen.

PERHAPS

*Once again, Hathach returned to Queen Esther with Mordecai's
message. In turn she sent a reply back to Mordecai. Tell Mordecai,
"In preparation for my audience with the king, do this: gather together all
the Jews in Susa, and fast and pray for me. Intercede for me. For three days
and nights, abstain from all food and drink. My maids and I will join you in
this time. And after the three days, I will go in to the king and plead my
people's case, even though it means breaking the law. And if I die, then I die!"*
ESTHER 4:15–16 VOICE

Queen Esther was one tough cookie. Raised by her uncle Mordecai,
she learned to trust him and his wisdom. So when he encouraged her
to talk to the king about the secret plan to annihilate the Jews, she
chose to believe and trust Mordecai—and she acted. He is the one who
said these famous words to her: *"Perhaps you have been made queen
for such a time as this"* (Esther 4:14 VOICE).

Who are the encouragers in your life? Who are the ones to challenge you to step into your calling even if you have to do so scared?
Perhaps God has you on planet Earth now to grow your faith as you
make a difference in the lives of others.

●

*Father, I know You chose me to be here now. Show me
what Your plan is for my life. In Jesus' name I pray, amen.*

UNSHAKABLE CONFIDENCE

So now, beloved ones, stand firm and secure. Live your lives with an unshakable confidence. We know that we prosper and excel in every season by serving the Lord, because we are assured that our union with the Lord makes our labor productive with fruit that endures.

1 Corinthians 15:58 tpt

When you hold the shield of faith, you'll find the courage to stand strong regardless of what comes your way. There is freedom in knowing that you don't have to bow before the things that scare you and trigger your insecurities. You don't have to cower as you fear failure. You don't have to worry about being derailed. Instead, you can live with unshakable confidence that God is God and He will enable you to do what He created you to do!

Ask the Lord for the faith it takes to dive into the deep waters with Him. Open your eyes and ears to watch and listen for His leading. Let Him use your skills and talents fully and completely to do the work set before you. And trust that when you commit your ways to the Lord, your work is never wasted. Through Him, you're assured the ability to be useful and helpful for the kingdom of God!

Father, give me unshakable confidence so I can do Your work. Increase my faith as I trust You for my strength and direction. In Jesus' name I pray, amen.

BEING CONTENT WITH YOU

But all of you, leaders and followers alike, are to be down to earth with each other, for—God has had it with the proud, but takes delight in just plain people. So be content with who you are, and don't put on airs. God's strong hand is on you; he'll promote you at the right time. Live carefree before God; he is most careful with you.

1 Peter 5:5-7 msg

It takes a lot of faith to be content with yourself. It's not easy to feel good about who we are unless we intentionally take an eternal perspective, trusting that God doesn't make trash. So often, we try to fit in and work to look the right way or say the right things. We want to feel relevant. We crave acceptance by others, so we act like someone we decide is more acceptable—someone cooler. But that's not what God wants us to do. If He made each of us unique and different on purpose, why do we spend so much time trying to be like everyone else?

Today, why don't you be honest with the Lord and tell Him your struggles with self-confidence? Maybe just be completely blunt as you confess your greatest fears or gaping wounds. And why not invite Him to increase your confidence in who He made you to be?

Father, show me what You see when You look at me. In Jesus' name I pray, amen.

FIRM GRIP ON FAITH

Keep a cool head. Stay alert. The Devil is poised to pounce, and would like nothing better than to catch you napping. Keep your guard up. You're not the only ones plunged into these hard times. It's the same with Christians all over the world. So keep a firm grip on the faith. The suffering won't last forever. It won't be long before this generous God who has great plans for us in Christ—eternal and glorious plans they are!—will have you put together and on your feet for good. He gets the last word; yes, he does.

1 Peter 5:8–11 MSG

This is a powerful reminder of the importance of keeping a firm grip on our faith by choosing to rely on God for strength when the enemy comes at you. Decide He has your back rather than cowering in anxiety and keep your guard up and eyes open to see the enemy's traps. Trust the Lord will protect you, and stay alert by spending time in the Word and in prayer, learning what He says is true and right. This battle isn't forever. And all of these necessitate a belief in the sovereignty of God. They require a firm grip on faith.

Father, I need Your strength and courage to stay vigilant against the enemy's plans to take me out. Always help me stay alert and keep my shield of faith in front. In Jesus' name I pray, amen.

THE EFFECT OF JESUS

"There is no one else who has the power to save us, for there is only one name to whom God has given authority by which we must experience salvation: the name of Jesus." The council members were astonished as they witnessed the bold courage of Peter and John, especially when they discovered that they were just ordinary men who had never had religious training. Then they began to understand the effect Jesus had on them simply by spending time with him.

ACTS 4:12–13 TPT

Jesus changes lives. He has the ability to restore hope to the hopeless and worth to those who feel worthless. He heals the brokenhearted and gives confidence to try again. He loves the unlovable and forgives the unforgivable. And He offers peace in chaos to those who ask. Jesus is all-knowing and all-powerful, and His heart for you is always good. And it's through your faith in Him that all of these are accessed.

You don't have to be a seminary student or a Bible scholar. Your life up to now doesn't have to be marked by perfection and flawlessness. There are no requirements to meet or standards to live up to. In your ordinariness, you are exactly who Jesus wants. And it's through your faith in Him that your life will be beautifully affected by His goodness.

Father, take me and mold me and change me. Let Jesus affect my life in amazing ways! In His name I pray, amen.

GOD DID IT

Why are you so amazed, my fellow Israelites? Why are you staring at my friend and me as though we did this miracle through our own power or made this fellow walk by our own holiness? We didn't do this—God did! The God of Abraham, the God of Isaac, the God of Jacob—the God of our ancestors has glorified Jesus, God's servant—the same Jesus whom you betrayed and rejected in front of Pilate, even though Pilate was going to release Him.

Acts 3:12–13 VOICE

Let's be careful we don't take the Lord's credit. It's His and His alone. We may partner with God, being His hands and feet. We might speak out against evil and present truth to those who will listen. We may even persevere through tough times and create awe from our friends and family. But we know these feats are products of time with God and His light in our life. Maybe we walked them out, but He gave us the strength. He filled us with stamina. He ignited the desire. And we need to be sure we don't let our actions be exalted above the Lord's name. Let's be quick to give Him credit, telling others it's our faith in God that enables us.

Father, to You be the glory! Let my life point others to You! There's no doubt You can, and You will, and I'm grateful to be part of Your army! In Jesus' name I pray, amen.

THE CHALLENGE TO NOT PAY ATTENTION

Do not fear them or their words, son of man. Though you will dwell among the thistles and briars of their hostility, though their reactions will make you think you're sitting on scorpions, do not be afraid. Pay no attention to their threats, and don't let their glaring faces intimidate you. They are a rebellious lot.

EZEKIEL 2:6 VOICE

When mean-spirited words come your way, don't let them stick. When someone tries to upset you or make you feel *less than*, remember who God says you are. Through all the thorny situations life throws your way, stay focused on God's promises to protect you. When someone's actions bite and leave you hurting, don't entertain their threats. Instead, activate your faith and talk to God. Ask Him for the strength and wisdom to navigate the messiness. Ask Him for the right perspective so you're not intimidated by situations or people. Ask Him to occupy your thoughts with His goodness so you don't pay attention to the haters. And even more, ask the Lord to fill your heart with His peace and to remind you of the value you hold to the One who created you.

Father, not paying attention to those bent on discouraging me is a tall order. Sometimes I think more on their words of hate than any compliments that come my way. Help me stand in faith as I choose to believe You over them. In Jesus' name I pray, amen.

WHO IS GOD TO YOU?

Bless the Lord, my rock, who taught my hands how to fight,
who taught my fingers how to do battle! God is my loyal one,
my fortress, my place of safety, my rescuer, my shield, in whom
I take refuge, and the one who subdues people before me.

PSALM 144:1-2 CEB

Here's what's so awesome about today's verse: the psalmist gets it.
He truly understands the power of God in his life and knows who He
is. He sees His mighty hand at work and trusts in the ways God will
come through for him in the future. The writer's faith is strong and
resolved. Go back and read the verses above. Sit with each descriptor
of the Lord and find the ones that resonate the most with you right
now. Write them down and thank Him for being present in your life.
Tell God why His help means so much.

Don't let the world steal your heart and trust. They will promise
you many things but won't be able to deliver on them. At least not for
long. Let today's scripture sink deep into your bones as you realize
the awesome power and love God has for you. . .because He is all these
things for you too.

Father, what a powerful reminder of who You promise to be in
my life. Help me remember when life hits me in the gut. Show me
Your faithfulness when I need rescuing. In Jesus' name I pray, amen.

BOLD PRAYERS

*LORD, part your skies and come down! Touch the mountains
so they smoke! Flash lightning and scatter the enemy! Shoot your
arrows and defeat them! Stretch out your hand from above! Rescue
me and deliver me from deep water, from the power of strangers, whose
mouths speak lies, and whose strong hand is a strong hand of deception!*

PSALM 144:5-8 CEB

This is quite a prayer! Today's verse offers us a great example of someone desperate for the Lord's intervention. They need Him to step in and rescue. And even more, they are asking Him to be visible and show His mighty power for all to see. Can you imagine the confidence a prayer like this would take?

Friend, you can pray the same way. You don't have to pray soft and sweet prayers using flowery words. Your prayers don't have to follow a formula or sound lofty. They don't have to be laced with fake pleasantries and political correctness. No, no, no, instead, you have the freedom to pray bold prayers full of passionate pleas. You can share what is on your mind. And you can ask for anything. God already knows the depths of your heart, but He wants to hear from you. Take that step of faith and talk to the Lord with complete transparency. Nothing you say or share will ever change the way He feels about you.

*Father, thank You for letting me be honest
with You! In Jesus' name I pray, amen.*

SOMETHING TO SING ABOUT

For God's Word is something to sing about! He is true to his promises, his word can be trusted, and everything he does is reliable and right. The Lord loves seeing justice on the earth. Anywhere and everywhere you can find his faithful, unfailing love!

PSALM 33:4–5 TPT

The idea that God's Word is something to sing about is a beautiful way to explain it. The writer was moved and deeply delighted. It stuck with him enough to have an audible impact to anyone around. It was in his mind and literally on his lips. Yep, it connected to his heart.

The promises of God are worth humming a tune or singing at the tops of your lungs. They are worthy of our trust because the Word tells us of His reliability. In other words, God will do what He says He will do. The Lord is just, which means He is fair, which means His promises and commandments apply to everyone. We're equally loved and favored. And knowing this helps to grow our faith as we choose to believe God Himself is faithful and trustworthy.

Father, let me sing Your goodness every day. Let Your promises always be on my lips. Grow my faith as I commit to spending more time with You, learning to trust deeper in Your Word. Thank You for being faithful and kind. In Jesus' name I pray, amen.

WITH ALL HE'S GOT

*We're depending on G*od*; he's everything we need. What's more,*
our hearts brim with joy since we've taken for our own his holy name.
*Love us, G*od*, with all you've got—that's what we're depending on.*
PSALM 33:20–22 MSG

Do you believe that you can depend on God for anything and everything? When it all hits the fan, do you trust Him for help? When you're drowning in grief, is the Lord the one you cry out to? When you're overwhelmed as a wife or a mom, stressed out by lofty expectations, are you going to the Lord in prayer each day? Friend, can we really have faith that He will come through for us?

The answer is yes, and it all boils down to the magnitude of His love. It's because of it that we can know without question He'll always be the best option for meeting our needs. And the longer we're in relationship with Him, we will gain a profound understanding that God is everything we need. The Lord loves you with all He's got, and there is nothing you can do to change that!

Father, I am depending on Your love because I know I can't navigate
my days without it. I'm so desperate for Your mighty hand to guide
me as I walk out this life in faith. Love me with all You've got, Lord.
I can't do this without You! In Jesus' name I pray, amen.

IT TAKES GUTS
AND GRIT

*Pharaoh, Egypt's king, called for some of the Hebrew midwives. Their
names were Shiphrah and Puah. Listen closely. Whenever you are looking
after a Hebrew woman who is in labor and ready to deliver, if she gives birth
to a son, then kill the baby. If it is a daughter, then allow her to live. But the
midwives respected God more than they feared Pharaoh, so they did not
carry out the Egyptian king's command. Instead, they let all the boys live.*
EXODUS 1:15–17 VOICE

Can you even imagine being given this kind of order? Pharaoh was
terrified at the growing number of Israelites in Egypt, so he asked
these God-fearing midwives to control the population through mur-
der. What confidence in God these women must have had to activate
their faith over their fear and disobey a direct order from the highest
official in the land.

It takes grit and guts to stand up for God over man. Doing what we
know is right is downright hard at times because we're afraid of the
backlash. But when we trust the Lord more than anyone else, we will
find the courage to do the right thing. And in the end, God will bless it.

*Father, help me care more about obeying You than following orders that go
against Your heart. I want to honor people here, but never at the expense of
my faith or Your reputation. I need discernment. In Jesus' name I pray, amen.*

TRUSTING SCARED

But Moses said to the Lord, "My Lord, I've never been able to speak well, not yesterday, not the day before, and certainly not now since you've been talking to your servant. I have a slow mouth and a thick tongue." Then the Lord said to him, "Who gives people the ability to speak? Who's responsible for making them unable to speak or hard of hearing, sighted or blind? Isn't it I, the Lord? Now go! I'll help you speak, and I'll teach you what you should say." But Moses said, "Please, my Lord, just send someone else."
Exodus 4:10–13 ceb

Even after Moses saw the burning bush and watched God turn his staff into a snake and then back into a staff. Even after God caused him to have a skin condition and then removed it immediately. Even after all these signs and wonders, Moses still lacked faith.

We can all relate to times where we know that we know God has us, but our insecurities scream louder. Doubt often overpowers our memory of all the times the Lord came through. Listen up, friend. You can trust Him scared. You can white knuckle your faith and take the next step. And when you do, He will build your confidence and courage for the next step.

Father, I can relate to Moses. Forgive my doubt and bolster my faith so I don't let anything stop me from following Your leading. In Jesus' name I pray, amen.

PERSPECTIVE

I want to report to you, friends, that my imprisonment here has had the opposite of its intended effect. Instead of being squelched, the Message has actually prospered. All the soldiers here, and everyone else, too, found out that I'm in jail because of this Messiah. That piqued their curiosity, and now they've learned all about him. Not only that, but most of the followers of Jesus here have become far more sure of themselves in the faith than ever, speaking out fearlessly about God, about the Messiah.
PHILIPPIANS 1:12–14 MSG

Paul had to be giggling with joy as he wrote this letter. What a crazy turn of events. His imprisonment, meant to quash the Gospel, actually caused it to spread! This is a great reminder that what we see in the natural is rarely what's happening in the spirit. In other words, when things look bleak, it might be the exact situation God will use to capture someone's heart for Him. Our job is to have faith to trust Him no matter what. Even more, let our faith remind us that we are not the Lord. It will keep us from trying to control or manipulate the outcome. The last thing we want to do is interfere with the God who promises to use all things for our benefit and His glory. Amen?

Father, I love knowing that Your will cannot be undone or undermined. Praise be to You in all things! In Jesus' name I pray, amen.

NEVER GIVE UP ON YOU

*"Even if the mountains were to crumble and the hills disappear,
my heart of steadfast, faithful love will never leave you, and my
covenant of peace with you will never be shaken," says Yahweh,
whose love and compassion will never give up on you.*

ISAIAH 54:10 TPT

Chances are your heart is broken just thinking about the people who have given up on you. Maybe it was a husband who walked away from your marriage or a parent who abandoned you, leaving you to figure things out alone. Maybe you were wrongfully fired from a job, a friend turned on you for choosing to speak out truth, or you were the one to tap out of a relationship you thought was forever. This is something every one of us can understand because it knits us together as humans.

But here is the good news: you are never in danger of God walking away from you. He says there is nothing—not one single thing ever—that could cause Him to give up on you. It's His deep love and compassion that seals that deal tight. The challenge is for you to believe it and accept it as truth. Reread today's verse and let it sink in.

*Father, it's hard to believe there's nothing I can do to make You
leave me. My life is full of people who've abandoned me for one
thing or another. Help me believe You. In Jesus' name I pray, amen.*

THIS IS YOUR HERITAGE

But no weapon that is formed against you shall prosper, and every tongue that shall rise against you in judgment you shall show to be in the wrong. This [peace, righteousness, security, triumph over opposition] is the heritage of the servants of the Lord [those in whom the ideal Servant of the Lord is reproduced]; this is the righteousness or the vindication which they obtain from Me [this is that which I impart to them as their justification], says the Lord.

ISAIAH 54:17 AMPC

What a powerful truth to hold on to when the storms of life begin to swirl around us. Sometimes we stare evil in the eyes, scared to death it will win. We watch trouble surface in our relationships and don't know how to stop it. We see lies come against us, and we worry how we'll defend ourselves. And we watch those we trust turn against us, often out of the blue. In our sadness, we feel stuck trying to work through the situation. What do we do? We cling to the Lord, who makes us a profound promise of protection and vindication.

Your heritage is peace, righteousness, security, and triumph over opposition. He promises to keep you safe. Let your faith secure this truth in your heart.

Father, I'm grateful to know You are in control and will take care of me. Give me the confidence to trust You and the faith to stand firm. In Jesus' name I pray, amen.

SLEEP LIKE A BABY

You will sleep like a baby, safe and sound—your rest will be sweet
and secure. You will not be subject to terror, for it will not terrify you.
Nor will the disrespectful be able to push you aside, because God is your
confidence in times of crisis, keeping your heart at rest in every situation.
Proverbs 3:24–26 TPT

When was the last time you slept like a baby? Chances are it was years ago, and these days sleep is more elusive than anything else. Night seems to be the time our brains won't shut off. It's when we process our frustrations from the day before or map out our upcoming busy day, whether we want to or not. It's those wee hours in the morning when our fears and insecurities become larger than life and we can't seem to find peace.

God is there with you, ready to hear what's heavy on your heart. He knows every detail about those things keeping you stirred up. He understands the complexity of them and how they intersect with your life. Even more, God has the ability to calm your anxious heart and comfort you. Tell Him what's bothering you, and then sleep like a baby.

Father, it's the middle of the night when I can't shut my mind off. In my fear,
I predict horrible outcomes and endings that leave me feeling hopeless
and fearful. Please comfort me. In Jesus' name I pray, amen.

EMPOWERED BY WISDOM AND DISCERNMENT

My child, never drift off course from these two goals for your life: to walk in wisdom and to discover discernment. Don't ever forget how they empower you. For they strengthen you inside and out and inspire you to do what's right; you will be energized and refreshed by the healing they bring. They give you living hope to guide you, and not one of life's tests will cause you to stumble.

PROVERBS 3:21–23 TPT

You'll receive great power by choosing to walk in wisdom and discernment. The Word says these two are important enough to be considered goals for your life because they are so beneficial. They not only give you inner strength, but that strength becomes something that inspires you to do the right thing. Even more, wisdom and discernment will energize you to live well, be guardrails as you walk it out, and bring healing all at the same time.

Ask the Father to give you these in spades. Ask Him every morning before your feet hit the floor, and in every situation where you have a choice to make. There's too much at stake to rely only on your humanity, flawed and limited. This life requires confidence in God as you navigate the ups and downs.

Father, please give me wisdom and discernment to live my one and only life well. I want to stay in Your will and walk with You daily. In Jesus' name I pray, amen.

GOD EQUIPS

This is the kind of confidence we have in and through the Anointed toward our God. Don't be mistaken; in and of ourselves we know we have little to offer, but any competence or value we have comes from God. Now God has equipped us to be capable servants of the new covenant, not by authority of the written law which only brings death, but by the Spirit who brings life.

2 Corinthians 3:4–6 voice

Don't think it's all up to you. Doing God's work in the world requires His help. We are plagued by human limitations that can't be overcome. We can't just try harder or work longer. When the Lord created you for good works, that also came with a guarantee that He'd give you the help needed to make it happen. It's God who equips you—Him alone.

Be careful not to put performance pressure on yourself. Instead, be quick to ask Him for what you're needing. Is it strength for the hard conversation? Patience as you raise kids? Confidence as you share your testimony? Forgiveness for the one who wronged you? Love for someone who doesn't deserve it? Lean on God and expect His help. He won't let you down.

Father, thank You for promising to equip me for the call You've placed on my life. I need Your help to make it happen, so please fill me with faith in Your promises. In Jesus' name I pray, amen.

YOUR TOMORROW
BELONGS TO GOD

Listen, those of you who are boasting, "Today or tomorrow we'll go to another city and spend some time and go into business and make heaps of profit!" But you don't have a clue what tomorrow may bring. For your fleeting life is but a warm breath of air that is visible in the cold only for a moment and then vanishes! Instead you should say, "Our tomorrows are in the Lord's hands and if he is willing we will live life to its fullest and do this or that."

JAMES 4:13–15 TPT

We are, by nature, planners. As women, we want to get our weekly schedules in place, so we know what's coming. We like predictability. We crave organization. And it brings us a sense of calm to think we have things in order, prepared and ready to go. But your tomorrow belongs to God.

Today's verses challenge us to hold loosely to our plans. There's nothing wrong with looking forward to the future and scheduling things. We'd be crazy not to, especially if we're trying to organize the details surrounding work and family commitments. But let's trust God's calendar for our life more. And if He has something else planned, let's trust Him as He rearranges our days.

Father, help me keep my plans in perspective so if You change them, I can go with the flow, trusting Your ways over mine. In Jesus' name I pray, amen.

SECURED AND UNSHAKEN

The Lord is my revelation-light to guide me along the way;
he's the source of my salvation to defend me every day. I fear no one!
I'll never turn back and run from you, Lord; surround and protect me.
When evil ones come to destroy me, they will be the ones who turn back.
My heart will not be afraid even if an army rises to attack. I know
that you are there for me, so I will not be shaken.

PSALM 27:1–3 TPT

We can always count on David to be super transparent with his emotions. His rawness with the Lord is so beautiful, and it shows us we can be the same way too. There's no good reason to hide our heart from God, and there is no evidence to ever suggest He turns away from us when we do. You're fully loved, and the Lord is protective of you.

In those times when you feel attacked by others, bare your heart before Him. Trust God with your mess. Open up about all your overwhelming feelings, unpacking in detail what is troubling and painful. In faith, run to Him rather than running away in shame or fear. It's God's love that will keep you secured and unshaken.

Father, I confess there are times I turn from You in shame.
Give me the confidence to know You love me no matter what
and are always there to help. In Jesus' name I pray, amen.

FEARLESS CONFIDENCE

Do not, therefore, fling away your [fearless] confidence, for it has a glorious and great reward. For you have need of patient endurance [to bear up under difficult circumstances without compromising], so that when you have carried out the will of God, you may receive and enjoy to the full what is promised.
HEBREWS 10:35–36 AMP

If you don't have courage, ask for it. Through God, it's available to you at all times. And if it seems you've lost the courage you once had, ask the Lord to restore it. You will need it in this life. It's what empowers you to make the right decision, speak up for truth, hold firm in your faith, try again, and be who He created you to be. Courage is part of every decision.

Every day, choose to be a woman of fearless confidence in the Lord. Know with every fiber of your being that God will always give you what you need to endure whatever life throws your way. Trust His plan. Because when you do, there is a beautiful blessing on the other side. Remember, courage is yours for the asking. It's a benefit of faith.

Father, life is hard and so often I want to hide away rather than deal with it. I'm tired from the fight and frustrated in my lack of perseverance. Honestly, sometimes I'm just downright scared because of what I'm facing. Please give me fearless confidence in You. In Jesus' name I pray, amen.

A FLOOD OF CONFIDENCE AND STRENGTH

Confidence and strength flood the hearts of the lovers of God who live in awe of him, and their devotion provides their children with a place of shelter and security.

PROVERBS 14:26 TPT

When you live strong in your faith, something amazing happens. It's a supernatural deposit of confidence and strength. It doesn't trickle into your life; scripture says it floods. Can you see that powerful visual? It's a reminder of abundance to those who love God. He blesses lavishly. And it is that confidence and strength that provide a sense of security. Your faith comes with benefits too awesome to imagine. The Lord never promises you an easy, carefree life, but He does fill you with courageous faith as you navigate it.

But it gets better. God promises that your obedience and belief not only blesses you, but it also provides protection for the next generation. So your willingness to trust the Lord and follow His plan for your life today has far-reaching gains others will receive in the future. Think of how much power your faith could have. It could be a generational blessing passed down for years to come!

Father, I am in awe of Your generosity and kindness for not only me but my children. Thank You for caring about the family of the faithful. Please flood my heart with Your confidence and strength so I can live and love well. In Jesus' name I pray, amen.

PRAYING FOR OTHERS

We always thank God for all of you when we mention you constantly in our prayers. This is because we remember your work that comes from faith, your effort that comes from love, and your perseverance that comes from hope in our Lord Jesus Christ in the presence of our God and Father. Brothers and sisters, you are loved by God, and we know that he has chosen you.

1 Thessalonians 1:2–4 ceb

Paul sets a powerful precedent in this letter written to the Thessalonian church. He lets them know that he prays for them constantly. He recognized their work and faith, their effort and love, and their perseverance and hope. While they may not have been in the same city, they were working together as a team to spread the Gospel of Jesus. And knowing this knitted Paul's heart together with theirs. Because of this, Paul was compelled to pray.

Do you pray for others? Regardless of whether you're working together for a common purpose or not, the practice of praying for one another is weighty. When you do, you're literally placing that person at the throne of God, trusting them to His hand. And it's a loving way to demonstrate your faith.

Father, right now I want to pray for these certain people. I believe You already know their needs, and I trust You to intervene as only You can. Save them. Heal them. Provide for them. In Jesus' name I pray, amen.

SUPPLEMENTING YOUR FAITH

So devote yourselves to lavishly supplementing your faith with goodness, and to goodness add understanding, and to understanding add the strength of self-control, and to self-control add patient endurance, and to patient endurance add godliness, and to godliness add mercy toward your brothers and sisters, and to mercy toward others add unending love.

2 PETER 1:5–7 TPT

God is asking you to continue working on your faith. It's not a one-and-done decision. Instead, it's a choice you make every day. Your faith is active, alive, and ever evolving. And His desire is that you add on to it as you mature in your belief.

How do you do this? You spend time in the Word, letting scripture sink deep into your heart. You spend time in prayer and dialogue with Him daily. You become part of the process and not part of the problem, always seeking God's guidance through the ups and downs of life rather than playing victim. And you invite Him to use your story—your life—as an encouragement to others. When you do, the Lord will increase your faith in beautiful ways that will benefit you and give glory to Him.

Father, I love that faith has no limits. I love that Your desire is for us to continue growing in relationship with You. And I love that You take an active role in making us more like Christ. In Jesus' name I pray, amen.

YOU ARE CHOSEN
AND CLAIMED

For this reason, beloved ones, be eager to confirm and validate that God has invited you to salvation and claimed you as his own. If you do these things, you will never stumble. As a result, the kingdom's gates will open wide to you as God choreographs your triumphant entrance into the eternal kingdom of our Lord and Savior, Jesus the Messiah.

2 Peter 1:10–11 TPT

God chose you to be His. Think about that for a moment. He created you just as He wanted you. He thought you up specially and wasn't in a bad mood when He did. You weren't an afterthought or a rush job. You're an intentional creation—a woman made on purpose and for a purpose. And your belief in Jesus as His Son who died for your sins seals eternity with Him.

Life will try to make you second-guess your faith. It will bring into question your belief system. And it will offer you false saviors, making all sorts of promises it can't deliver. But your job is to hold on to the truth of who you are and who God is. White knuckle your faith if you must, but remember you're chosen and claimed.

Father, thank You for choosing me. Sometimes I forget who I am and whose I am, and I need reminders I am important. I need reminders that I'm claimed and chosen by the One who created me. In Jesus' name I pray, amen.

YOUR PRAYER ADVOCATE

Meanwhile, the moment we get tired in the waiting, God's Spirit is right alongside helping us along. If we don't know how or what to pray, it doesn't matter. He does our praying in and for us, making prayer out of our wordless sighs, our aching groans. He knows us far better than we know ourselves, knows our pregnant condition, and keeps us present before God. That's why we can be so sure that every detail in our lives of love for God is worked into something good.
ROMANS 8:26–28 MSG

Did you know the Holy Spirit provides prayer support? When we find ourselves without the right words, the Spirit intervenes on our behalf. He interprets our mumbled and jumbled words and thoughts to God, making sense when we can't. In those times we aren't able to describe our pain, He will. When we can't explain our feelings, the Spirit does it for us. He knows us better than we know ourselves, and that makes Him the perfect prayer advocate when we need help.

So have faith in knowing God will get the whole picture of your needs. He will fully understand the complexity of your situation. He won't be confused or missing vital details. The Holy Spirit will make sure of it.

Father, thank You for the Holy Spirit's role in my prayer life. I rest knowing I have a prayer advocate who ensures God knows the details. In Jesus' name I pray, amen.

WALKING OUT YOUR FAITH

Speak blessing, not cursing, over those who reject and persecute you.
Celebrate with those who celebrate, and weep with those who grieve.
Live happily together in a spirit of harmony, and be as mindful of
another's worth as you are your own. Don't live with a lofty mind-set,
thinking you are too important to serve others, but be willing to do
menial tasks and identify with those who are humble minded.
Don't be smug or even think for a moment that you know it all.
ROMANS 12:14–16 TPT

Today's scripture offers a perfect snapshot of what it looks like to walk out your faith. This isn't everything, but it's enough to prove you'll need the Lord's help to do it well. Too often, we decide we can live right on our own. We don't see the need to involve God in the nitty-gritty details because we think we're fully capable alone. But then we run across verses like these and we realize we need help!

Reread this passage in Romans and make note of what stands out. Where do you need God's help most? What seems almost impossible without the Lord's support? What part will require you to activate your faith without fail? There's no shame or blame intended. Instead, let's realize how desperately we need God to help us walk out our faith.

Father, the reality is I need You to help me
live a faith-filled life. In Jesus' name I pray, amen.

HIS FIERCENESS OF PROTECTION AND CARE

Yahweh responds, "But how could a loving mother forget her nursing child and not deeply love the one she bore? Even if there is a mother who forgets her child, I could never, no never, forget you. Can't you see? I have carved your name on the palms of my hands! Your walls are always my concern."
ISAIAH 49:15–16 TPT

There is a powerful bond between a loving mother and child. There's a fierceness of protection and care that is unmatched. You've heard the term *mama bear*, indicating that if you mess with her baby, you'll get the full set of claws and teeth in response. Maybe you were raised by one. Maybe you are one.

God is making a point. He is trying to instill an unshakable sense of security in you. He's making a case that He will never walk away, hoping you will choose to trust His fierceness of protection and care. The Lord has even carved your name on His palm as a constant reminder. Part of having faith means you make a choice to believe what God says is true and real. Today, settle in your heart that the Lord fully and completely loves you and will never forget you.

Father, I am choosing to embrace the truth of who I am to You. I am choosing to believe Your promise to never forget me is unwavering as well. What a gift! In Jesus' name I pray, amen.

SAFE-HARBOR GOD

My help and glory are in God—granite-strength
and safe-harbor-God—So trust him absolutely, people;
lay your lives on the line for him. God is a safe place to be.
PSALM 62:7-8 MSG

This means that when you've been excluded from the group, you can share that pain with God. When your parent gets a scary health diagnosis, He will be there to comfort you. Every time that old wound gets poked by someone's words, the Lord is ready to listen. When your marriage feels like it's crumbling or you're tired of being single, God is a safe place to purge your fears. In those times where you're worried about your kids, He is there to offer strength and perspective. Your faith in God unlocks His power in your life.

How would life be more manageable if you leaned on Him in those tough moments? What keeps you from trusting the Lord? What would need to change so you could? When you make the decision to put your hope in God, that act of faith ignites a peace in your heart. It gives you strength to respond. It gives you wisdom and discernment to navigate the next steps. It gives you a sense of His presence to remind you you're not alone. Let God be your safe-harbor God through every storm you face.

Father, give me the confidence and courage to be
quicker to ask for Your help. In Jesus' name I pray, amen.

ALIVE AND ACTIVE

For the word of God is living and active and full of power [making it operative, energizing, and effective]. It is sharper than any two-edged sword, penetrating as far as the division of the soul and spirit [the completeness of a person], and of both joints and marrow [the deepest parts of our nature], exposing and judging the very thoughts and intentions of the heart.

Hebrews 4:12 amp

God's Word is mysterious because while it was written thousands of years ago, it still holds relevance in your life. Somehow, it still provides insight and understanding to the situations you're facing today. It unlocks time-tested truths that matter in the here and now. It's living and active, convicting and encouraging when we need it the most. It holds power to meet us right where we are and give us a word of hope. It exposes sin, affirms choices, and provides direction. It affirms our worth. It settles our identity. And it opens our eyes to the will and ways of the Lord, teaching us more about the God we serve.

Let His Word be alive and active in your life. Spend time reading it every day, asking Him to speak to you through it. And watch your faith grow.

Father, I'm in awe of the power I can receive through the Bible. It's a living document that shows Your love and care for Your children. And I'm blessed by it! In Jesus' name I pray, amen.

BENEFITS OF LOVING BIG

*When you live a life of abandoned love, surrendered before
the awe of God, here's what you'll experience: Abundant life.
Continual protection. And complete satisfaction!*

Proverbs 19:23 TPT

Choose to be the kind of woman who loves big. Be lavish and reckless, making sure your friends and family know how you feel about them. Love is so powerful, that when we are secure in it, we're able to step out in confidence and courage. We feel bolstered by it. It's the foundation that keeps us surefooted.

In the same vein, make sure God feels your unrestricted love for Him too. Be generous in your praise. Be extravagant in your gratitude for all He's done. Let the Lord feel your abundant appreciation. Make sure He knows the depths of your reverence for who He is. Be quick to share God-moments with others, giving Him due credit for intervening. Don't let a day pass without sharing your thankfulness for meeting your every need, every time. This will not only set you up for blessings, but it will also supernaturally increase your faith. Remembering His goodness trains us to trust He will do it again.

*Father, I see the ways You've intersected with my life and I am so grateful for it.
I love You big, and I wanted to make sure You knew it. I don't just love You for
what You've done. I love You for who You are. In Jesus' name I pray, amen.*

YOU CAN'T SAVE YOURSELF

No king succeeds with a big army alone, no warrior wins by brute strength. Horsepower is not the answer; no one gets by on muscle alone. Watch this: God's eye is on those who respect him, the ones who are looking for his love. He's ready to come to their rescue in bad times; in lean times he keeps body and soul together.

PSALM 33:16–19 MSG

What a compelling passage of scripture reminding us that we can't save ourselves. Sure, we have power and strength. Yes, we can train our bodies to be strong and our minds to be smart. We may have a mama-bear mom or an overprotective dad as allies. We might have a group of friends who would come to our rescue or support us no matter what. But friend, the psalmist is shining a spotlight of reality through his words.

The truth is that our humanity will only take us so far and we will eventually get to the end of us. And while we have community to help us, we have a deep need for God. Our faith kicks in when we realize He is a necessity for living with purpose and passion.

●

Father, I get so frustrated at how quickly I forget how much I need You. I waste so much time trying to do it all myself. Help me go to You first instead of as a last resort. In Jesus' name I pray, amen.

BIG ASKS

Jabez was more honorable than his brothers; but his mother named him Jabez, saying, "Because I gave birth to him in pain." Jabez cried out to the God of Israel, saying, "Oh that You would indeed bless me and enlarge my border [property], and that Your hand would be with me, and You would keep me from evil so that it does not hurt me!" And God granted his request.

1 Chronicles 4:9–10 amp

Jabez had the gumption to ask God for more. He asked to be blessed with an increase in land and for protection from evil. It was his faith that allowed him to boldly ask for big things. Jabez was secure in his request because he knew the power of his God. In confidence, he dreamed big and asked the Lord for what he wanted. And what happened? God granted his request.

Let's keep in mind that God is predictably unpredictable. Asking never guarantees a yes answer. He sees the bigger picture and knows exactly what we need. So if His response to your request is a no or a not now, let your faith be strong enough to trust His timing and plan.

Father, thank You for the freedom to ask for anything. I appreciate knowing I can dream big dreams and take them to You. But I'm also grateful for Your knowledge to know what's best for me. Give me the confidence to trust Your answer either way. In Jesus' name I pray, amen.

HE WILL TEACH
YOU TO PRAY

One day he was praying in a certain place. When he finished, one of his disciples said, "Master, teach us to pray just as John taught his disciples." So he said, "When you pray, say, Father, reveal who you are. Set the world right. Keep us alive with three square meals. Keep us forgiven with you and forgiving others. Keep us safe from ourselves and the Devil."

LUKE 11:1–4 MSG

Just like the disciples did, you too can ask God to teach you to pray. Not that there is any formula to follow or any right way to pray, but sometimes we need help expanding our prayers because we aren't sure how to make that happen.

Think about it. Do you feel your prayer life is stagnant? Do you feel stuck in the same rut with it, not sure how to say what you're really feeling? Are you ever bored with your prayers because they feel flat? While it's true we have the Holy Spirit interceding for us, your prayer life is meant to be fulfilling. So if you want to make some positive changes, ask the Lord to show you how to pray. Ask Him to teach you new and fresh ways to connect with Him in prayer.

Father, will You help me pray with more passion and purpose? Give me inspiration. Give me creativity. Open my mind so I can learn new ways to communicate with You. In Jesus' name I pray, amen.

A CHANGED LIFE

Jesus came back, "God bless you, Simon, son of Jonah! You didn't get that answer out of books or from teachers. My Father in heaven, God himself, let you in on this secret of who I really am. And now I'm going to tell you who you are, really are. You are Peter, a rock. This is the rock on which I will put together my church, a church so expansive with energy that not even the gates of hell will be able to keep it out."

MATTHEW 16:17–18 MSG

What an extraordinary moment for Peter. It was because of his faith that Jesus changed him in an instant. He took a fisherman and made him a disciple. And in this moment, He took a disciple and empowered him to carry a powerful mantle of responsibility. Something remarkable happens when the Lord reveals His plan for your life. When He tells you who He created you to be, something shifts in your spirit.

It takes spiritual eyes and ears trained on God to see and hear Him. It takes faith to know His still, small voice through a boisterous world. But when you make space for a relationship with the Lord and it becomes a priority, He will call you by name and tell you who you are. And it will change your life.

*Father, I appreciate the ways You empower me
to live a faith-filled life. In Jesus' name I pray, amen.*

THE CASE FOR FAITH-FILLED LIVING

Oh, it will be so bad for you, My rebellious children, who enact a plan
but not as I would have you do, who form an alliance contrary
to My Spirit, compounding sin, one bad choice after another.

ISAIAH 30:1 VOICE

What a compelling reason to live a life of faith. Rebellious living only leads us in the opposite direction from God. It's not about perfection, but rather purposeful living. It's choosing to be obedient to what the Lord is asking and trying to follow the path of righteousness instead of always looking to satisfy the flesh. This kind of living means your heart is turned toward God and you want to please Him with how You live. You want your actions and words to point others to the Father in heaven. It's a choice to love the Lord with all your heart, your mind, and your life.

Where are you rebellious right now? Where are you making destructive decisions that don't lead to righteous living? What is keeping you from activating your faith and asking God for help? Friend, He knows we all need His strength to walk out this life according to His purpose. Ask Him for what you need.

Father, I don't want to be rebellious. I don't want to make bad choices.
Instead, I want to live a life full of faith and trust in You. Would
You help me live that way? In Jesus' name I pray, amen.

PRAYING FOR WISDOM

A wise person is careful in all things and turns quickly from evil,
while the impetuous fool moves ahead with overconfidence.

Proverbs 14:16 tpt

Pray for wisdom. Every day ask the Lord to show you the right way from the wrong way. Ask for discernment to know good from not so good and tell Him you're committed to seeking truth. In prayer, activate your faith by surrendering your desires, telling God to lead the way. Be mindful in your choices. And friend, when you get a gut feeling that something's not right, have the courage to turn from it.

Part of our journey is learning to see God moving in our life. We have to train our eyes and ears on Him, becoming sensitive to His leading. It's a vital part of maturing in the faith. Today, talk to God about the places you need His wisdom. Share with the Lord where you need discernment. And ask Him to graciously fill you with truth so you can avoid being overconfident in ways that are nothing but foolish.

Father, I know I've made so many bad decisions that have led me down the wrong path. I confess I often rely on my own wisdom instead of seeking Yours. My relationship with You is important to me, and I want my decisions to glorify Your holy name. Please help me know the difference between right and wrong. Please give me wisdom. In Jesus' name I pray, amen.

WHAT TO THINK ABOUT

From now on, brothers and sisters, if anything is excellent and if anything is admirable, focus your thoughts on these things: all that is true, all that is holy, all that is just, all that is pure, all that is lovely, and all that is worthy of praise. Practice these things: whatever you learned, received, heard, or saw in us. The God of peace will be with you.

Philippians 4:8–9 CEB

The Lord knows how our minds can start down rabbit trails that lead us to horrible outcomes and endings. We think about all the ways we've failed. . .and will again. We focus on what scares us, certain it's going to take us out. We entertain insecurities and how we don't measure up to the world's standards. We replay conversations that remind us why we're choosing not to forgive, stirring up bitterness and anger once again. Bottom line: it diminishes our faith.

That's why God wants us to think on things that are admirable, excellent, true, holy, just, pure, lovely, and worthy of praise. We should practice these thoughts, meaning be quick to bring our minds back to them when the rabbit trails begin to form. In faith, we're to make an intentional choice about the content of our thoughts.

Father, I will need Your help with this one. Sometimes my mind is so out of control. Help me be aware of my thoughts enough to redirect them when needed. In Jesus' name I pray, amen.

YOU ARE KNOWN

For You shaped me, inside and out. You knitted me together in my mother's womb long before I took my first breath. I will offer You my grateful heart, for I am Your unique creation, filled with wonder and awe. You have approached even the smallest details with excellence; Your works are wonderful; I carry this knowledge deep within my soul.
PSALM 139:13–14 VOICE

It's pretty amazing to realize what these verses are telling you—that God has played an integral part in your creation. He managed every detail. You matter so much to the Lord that He was 100 percent involved with you from the very beginning. He knew exactly who He wanted you to be and made it so. Let that sink in for a moment.

So friend, since He has been a hands-on God to you from the start, it should bolster your confidence in who He can be for you today. It should make your faith in Him blossom. It should shatter every barrier that keeps you from fully trusting God's hand in your life. You are known and loved. Invite Him into the details of today.

●

Father, I'm so grateful You know every detail of me. How amazing that You were knitting me together in my mother's womb. You took time to create me. Let that increase my faith and build a beautiful relationship of trust in You! In Jesus' name I pray, amen.

WE NEED HELP

Post this at all the intersections, dear friends: Lead with your ears,
follow up with your tongue, and let anger straggle along in the rear.
God's righteousness doesn't grow from human anger. So throw all spoiled
virtue and cancerous evil in the garbage. In simple humility, let our gardener,
God, landscape you with the Word, making a salvation-garden of your life.
JAMES 1:19–21 MSG

If we're to be slow to speak and quick to listen, let's agree we need God's help. If James is saying that anger shouldn't be our first response to hurtful and frustrating situations, let's acknowledge that our chances are hopeless without the Lord. Our intentions may be good, but our humanity gets in the way sometimes. We may be awesome, but we're not that awesome.

That's why this passage goes on to tell us how desperately we need Him to be involved. We need God to landscape us with His Word so we can spotlight Him with our words and actions. We need to activate our faith so we can live and love well. And when we do, God will give us the ability to lead with our ears and not our mouths and keep anger in its place.

Father, I admit my need for Your intervention. I simply cannot walk
this passage of scripture out without You. Work in my heart so it stays
focused on responding to others in the right ways. In Jesus' name I pray, amen.

HOW TO LOVE AND PRAY FOR YOUR ENEMIES

"You have heard that it was said, You must love your neighbor and hate your enemy. But I say to you, love your enemies and pray for those who harass you so that you will be acting as children of your Father who is in heaven. He makes the sun rise on both the evil and the good and sends rain on both the righteous and the unrighteous."
MATTHEW 5:43–45 CEB

Holy moly, this is a tough passage of scripture. Why? Because it's asking us to do something that doesn't come easily. It goes against what our flesh wants. Think about it. When someone hurts you, is your first response to love them? When your kids are bullied at school, your husband loses his job, your aging parents are scammed, or your friend is assaulted, do you want to go hug the perpetrators? It's easy to love the lovable, but it's a whole different story to love the unlovable and pray for them.

We can only do this through faith. We must ask God to let us see them through His eyes. We need the Lord to put love in our heart for them. We have to be intentional to open ourselves up to His transformation.

Father, this is a hard one for me. I desperately need You to change my heart so I can walk this out in my life. In Jesus' name I pray, amen.

GOD WILL SETTLE THE SCORE

Don't ever say, "I'll get you for that!"
Wait for God; he'll settle the score.
PROVERBS 20:22 MSG

Have you ever enjoyed plotting revenge? Let's just be honest: there are situations and people who have hurt us so badly, and we've all entertained ideas of getting them back. Maybe it was a conversation we practiced out loud where we stood up for ourselves and said the things we wished we'd said. Maybe we thought up ways to get the gossip train rolling so others would know what really happened. It's our human nature to want to defend ourselves and those we love.

But when we do, we're squashing our faith in the Lord. He is clear in His Word that He's the Judge and will be the One to settle the score. We must choose to trust His timing and ways. And honestly, sometimes it's a hard pill to swallow. Ask God to give you patience and fill you with peace. Ask the Lord to settle your spirit and calm your anxious heart, believing that He has complete understanding of the situation and will come through.

Father, I confess that I want to fight. I want to exact revenge on those who have hurt me or someone I love. I want to spill the truth and discredit others. I want to make them pay. Please grow my faith in You, trusting You will settle the score. In Jesus' name I pray, amen.

THE CALL TO LOVE, NOT SLANDER

Dear friends, as part of God's family, never speak against another family member, for when you slander a brother or sister you violate God's law of love. And your duty is not to make yourself a judge of the law of love by saying that it doesn't apply to you, but your duty is to obey it!

JAMES 4:11 TPT

Since God has asked us—commanded us—to love others, we can't use our words against them. Our heart toward them should always be good. We should care about protecting their reputation and name. And that means that we should shut down any gossip we hear from others as well.

Love always protects. It keeps no record of wrongs. It always hopes. Remember this when tempted to talk badly about someone. Maybe they did wrong. Maybe they were hurtful, and it only seems fair to denounce them. But your faith would dictate taking those unkind thoughts to God instead of your bestie. You can say all the things that need to be said, but only to Him. He's the perfect sounding board who not only brings peace to your heart but also judges any wrongdoing.

Father, I have broken this command a million times. Thank You for forgiveness. Would You please help me remember that You are a safe place to share what's really in my heart? That then frees me up to honor and respect others. In Jesus' name I pray, amen.

WHOM WILL YOU SERVE?

"It is impossible for a person to serve two masters at the same time. You will be forced to love one and reject the other. One master will be despised and the other will have your loyal devotion. It is no different with God and the wealth of this world. You must enthusiastically love one and definitively reject the other."

LUKE 16:13 TPT

Every day, you have a choice to make when it comes to your faith. Will you serve God or your flesh? Will you prioritize time with the Lord, or will your priorities be focused on worldly things? Will you devote time to reading God's Word, or will you find your teachings from the world's offerings? Will you choose Christian living, or will you follow the trends of society? While these seem to invite clear-cut answers right now, it's a different story when you have to walk it out in real time.

Today, declare your allegiance to God above all else. Tell Him He's worthy of serving and why you're choosing Him. Confess where your priorities have been mixed up in the past. And ask for an increase of faith so you can have loyal devotion to your heavenly Father.

Father, thank You for Your patience with me. I confess I've served others instead of You, but I don't want to do that anymore. Give me the desire to love You above anyone and anything else. In Jesus' name I pray, amen.

BE BLESSED

Blessed are the meek and gentle—they will inherit the earth.
Blessed are those who hunger and thirst for righteousness—
they will be filled. Blessed are the merciful—they will be shown
mercy. Blessed are those who are pure in heart—they will see God.
Blessed are the peacemakers—they will be called children of God.
MATTHEW 5:5–9 VOICE

What a beautiful passage of scripture. It's so encouraging to see what attitudes specifically evoke a blessing, because they are very different from what society says are important. And even more, make sure you pay special attention to the fact that blessings come to those who choose the right things. This is never a call to be perfect. God is asking for you to live with purpose and passion.

When you choose to be gentle, seek righteous living, show mercy, or purpose to be pure and try to live at peace whenever possible, extraordinary blessings occur. Go back and reread to see what each choice yields. Which one affirms you the most? Which one challenges you the most? Then talk to God about it.

Father, what a great reminder that obedience comes with a blessing.
Thank You for rewarding the things that matter the most instead of
the things of little value to the kingdom. You are a blessing to me!
Help me be a blessing to others! In Jesus' name I pray, amen.

THE SHIFT

Where do you think all these appalling wars and quarrels come from?
Do you think they just happen? Think again. They come about because
you want your own way, and fight for it deep inside yourselves. You lust
for what you don't have and are willing to kill to get it. You want what
isn't yours and will risk violence to get your hands on it.

JAMES 4:1–2 MSG

When you become a faith-filled woman, your life will begin to shift. You'll see and feel it, and it will be such an encouragement to your heart. Your attention will naturally begin to change from being self-focused to others focused. You'll find yourself more willing to share your time and treasure with those in need. And your motivation will be things of heaven rather than what the world can offer. But unless you are intentional to grow in your faith, these things can fade.

Ask the Lord to keep you from falling back into old ways. Ask Him to continue to sharpen your faith and deepen your trust in Him. Ask that He keep your eyes focused on Him rather than lusting for the world's offerings. And invite Him to remove the part of you that craves selfishness and replace it with a generous spirit.

Father, I say yes and amen to wanting You above all else. Grow my faith
to focus on You and leave behind my old self. In Jesus' name I pray, amen.

LIVING DIFFERENTLY

Let all bitterness and wrath and anger and clamor [perpetual animosity,
resentment, strife, fault-finding] and slander be put away from you, along
with every kind of malice [all spitefulness, verbal abuse, malevolence].
Be kind and helpful to one another, tender-hearted [compassionate,
understanding], forgiving one another [readily and freely],
just as God in Christ also forgave you.
EPHESIANS 4:31–32 AMP

Keep in mind that your salvation is not connected to your works. You're saved by faith alone, believing Jesus is the Son of God and that He died on the cross for your sins. The Word is clear when it says we're saved by faith and not works. Let's settle that in our hearts.

But a by-product of faith is a desire to live and love differently. It's setting aside the ways you used to operate and embracing the ways of God. It's an intentional decision to see the world through the lens of love and grace. How do you get there? Start by investing time in your relationship with the Lord. That's where heart transformation begins. Then continue to choose God's way—ways like in today's verse—every chance you get.

Father, I am committed to growing in my relationship with You.
I want my words and actions to point to You in heaven. I want people
to notice the difference and ask about it so I can tell them all about You.
I'm so glad You chose me to be Yours. In Jesus' name I pray, amen.

A NEW LIFE

Don't lie to one another. You're done with that old life. It's like a
filthy set of ill-fitting clothes you've stripped off and put in the fire.
Now you're dressed in a new wardrobe. Every item of your new
way of life is custom-made by the Creator, with his label on it.
COLOSSIANS 3:9–10 MSG

It's so easy to lie, isn't it? Too often, they just roll off our tongue without a second thought. We can usually find a way to justify them, saying it really doesn't hurt anyone. We may lie so we don't have to attend a boring event or because we don't want to hurt someone's feelings. We may lie because it will get a family member out of an unwanted commitment. Regardless, we justify the lies and decide they are okay with God.

But Paul is calling us higher. He reminds us that lying—even if we think it's for a good reason—is part of our old self. And because of Jesus, we have the unique opportunity to leave that old habit behind for good. We can choose to stand in the truth with confidence.

Father, what an honor to be made new in You. Thank You for not
holding my past against me and instead trading it for a new life.
I won't take it for granted! In Jesus' name I pray, amen.

ASK FOR WHAT YOU NEED

Jesus said to him, "What do you want me to do for you?" The man
replied, "My Master, please, let me see again!" Jesus responded,
"Your faith heals you. Go in peace, with your sight restored."
All at once, the man's eyes opened and he could see again, and he
began at once to follow Jesus, walking down the road with him.

MARK 10:51-52 TPT

Can you even imagine how this man felt to have his eyesight restored? He went from darkness to light in a moment. And it was his faith in Jesus that healed him. He just chose to believe the Lord had the power and ability to change his life. And that trust made healing possible.

There are many parts of us that need healing. It may be a physical ailment, like a disease or a birth defect. It may be an injury we suffered. But we also need healing of the mind, especially when our thought life is full of negatives. We need emotional healing. Think of the times throughout life where you've felt worthless or unlovable, and how they've left scars on your heart. The truth is that we all need Jesus to restore us. And it all starts with faith.

Father, I love that You care enough to make me whole by healing
my brokenness. I need the kind of restoration only You can provide.
Please hear my cry for Your hand in my life! In Jesus' name I pray, amen.

WITHOUT PREJUDICE

My fellow believers, do not practice your faith in our
glorious Lord Jesus Christ with an attitude of partiality
[toward people—show no favoritism, no prejudice, no snobbery].
JAMES 2:1 AMP

While on earth, Jesus preached time and time again to love one another. He commanded it and made a case for it. He gave us the ability and beautiful and powerful examples of what it looks like to love those around you. Even more, Jesus gave His life on the cross to prove the Father's love. And He died for every single person without prejudice.

Let's live and love the same way. There's no room to pick and choose who is worthy of love and respect. We have all sinned and fallen short of God's glory. In His eyes, you are no better than anyone else and no one is more favored by God over you. It's an equal playing field. And because of your faith, your heart can be full of love for others too. Ask the Lord to let you see everyone through His eyes. Ask Him for compassion and empathy. And ask Him to remove any judgment that may be lingering in your heart.

Father, I want to be an agent of love in a world that beats people up.
Give me an open heart without favoritism and open eyes to always
see the best in those around me. In Jesus' name I pray, amen.

THE CONNECTION BETWEEN OUR HEART AND OUR WORDS

If you put yourself on a pedestal, thinking you have become a role model in all things religious, but you can't control your mouth, then think again. Your mouth exposes your heart, and your religion is useless.

JAMES 1:26 VOICE

Few things will ruin your witness more than an unrestrained tongue. When others know you're a woman of faith, they will watch how you respond to life. Make no mistake. How you live will preach one way or another—good or not so good. While God isn't expecting you to be perfect, others probably are. They're watching how you live and love. It may not be fair, but it's reality.

That's why James wrote this passage of scripture. It's such a powerful reminder that we need God to transform our heart because our words expose it. If we are full of love, we will speak lovely things. If we're full of faith, it will show in our words. If we're full of compassion, it will be evident in how we respond. There is a weighty connect between our heart and our words, and it should serve as the catalyst to deepen our relationship with the Lord.

Father, I know my time with You has direct results in how I live. Help me make quiet time a priority so I can be filled with Your love. Give me a pure heart so my words will reflect it. In Jesus' name I pray, amen.

PUTTING OTHERS FIRST

Don't push your way to the front; don't sweet-talk your way
to the top. Put yourself aside, and help others get ahead.
Don't be obsessed with getting your own advantage.
Forget yourselves long enough to lend a helping hand.
Philippians 2:3–4 msg

It's hard to put others first when we're consistently saturated by worldly messages telling us to do the opposite. Those messages remind us to take care of ourselves first. They encourage us to do what feels right to get ahead. And they are quick to inform us of the immeasurable value of looking out for number one. Pretty different from Paul's words in today's verse, right? And drastically different than how God wants us to live.

Let's activate our faith by choosing to walk out the Lord's heart for humanity. How? Live an honest life free from manipulation or ladder climbing. Be willing to help others find their footing, even if it means you lose ground in your own journey. Trust that God will promote you in His timing so it's not something that keeps you from focusing on the needs of others. When we align our heart with His, we can trust He will bless our obedience in beautiful ways.

Father, what a shift in perspective. Selfishness is so ingrained in society we
don't even notice it anymore. Thanks for the reminder that in Your economy,
last is first. Help me choose it in how I live. In Jesus' name I pray, amen.

CREATED FOR COMMUNITY

We have different gifts that are consistent with God's grace that has been given to us. If your gift is prophecy, you should prophesy in proportion to your faith. If your gift is service, devote yourself to serving. If your gift is teaching, devote yourself to teaching. If your gift is encouragement, devote yourself to encouraging. The one giving should do it with no strings attached. The leader should lead with passion. The one showing mercy should be cheerful.

Romans 12:6–8 ceb

You were created for community. We all were. When God created each of us, He took time to determine the exact giftings He'd bake in. He was intentional and specific, making sure not everyone received the same talents. Like today's passage of scripture reveals, we're each made differently on purpose and for a purpose. Because He knew that when we joined forces, the variety of abilities would fit together to make a beautiful and powerful community of believers to further the Word of God.

This is why we celebrate the diversity of God's family. Rather than try to mold one another, we can instead discover the giftings and help grow the roots of faith together.

Father, I'm so grateful to know I am an intentional creation full of talents You specifically determined just for me. That makes me feel so loved by You. Would You help me find them, embrace them, and have the confidence to share them with others? In Jesus' name I pray, amen.

PROOF OF YOUR WORTH

"What is the value of your soul to God? Could your worth be defined by an amount of money? God doesn't abandon or forget even the small sparrow he has made. How then could he forget or abandon you? What about the seemingly minor issues of your life? Do they matter to God? Of course they do! So you never need to worry, for you are more valuable to God than anything else in this world."

LUKE 12:6-7 TPT

Let the weight of this passage of scripture sink deep into your DNA. Reread it again, out loud. As women, don't we need this kind of reminder almost daily? The truth is, there's no shortage of people and situations quick to discount our value. There are plenty of opportunities to feel worthless every day. And isn't it just like our loving Father to want us to know the truth of who we are to Him?

These are words to cling to when the world punches us in the gut. It's so vital that we believe in our goodness. And understanding how much God loves us can be a huge faith builder. Today, tell the Lord about your insecurities. Share with Him what is hurting you. And ask Him to fill your heart with His love and acceptance of you.

●

Father, this is a painful conversation. I could really use a divine reminder of my value and worth in Your eyes. In Jesus' name I pray, amen.

STAND STRONG IN FAITH

Then the devil brought him to a very high mountain and showed him all the kingdoms of the world and their glory. He said, "I'll give you all these if you bow down and worship me." Jesus responded, "Go away, Satan, because it's written, You will worship the Lord your God and serve only him."

MATTHEW 4:8–10 CEB

Your faith matters, friend. It's important and it's powerful, and the enemy is going to do everything in his power to diminish it. Just like he tried with Jesus, he knows what to say that might sway you, but his promises are empty. His goal is for you to live broken and defeated, far apart from a relationship with God. Even he knows how central that connection is for you to feel strengthened, emboldened, and empowered, and he wants to shut it down.

No matter what comes your way, hold your faith tight and trust the Lord. Let Him build your confidence. Let God grow your courage and resolve. And when you feel the enemy begin to whisper discouragement, stand in your authority as a believer and command the devil to go away in the name of Jesus. It's because of Him you are that powerful. Wield that sword of faith and stand strong in the power given to you by God Himself!

Father, thank You that my faith affords me so many benefits in Your mighty name. In Jesus' name I pray, amen.

SCRIPTURE INDEX

Old Testament

New Testament